DARK FEMININE ENERGY FOR MANIFESTATION

The 7 Secrets
of Radiating Powerfully Seductive
Femme Fatale Energy to Magnetically Attract
Your Deepest Desires

DARK FEMININE ENERGY FOR MANIFESTATION

The 7 Secrets
of Radiating Powerfully Seductive
Femme Fatale Energy to Magnetically Attract
Your Deepest Desires

Seraphina Sinclair

Table of Contents

Introduction

Women are already strong; it's about changing the way the world perceives that strength.

–G. D. Anderson

In my youth, I was shy and very insecure. This resulted in me not being able to manifest everything I desired, like being sportier and more outgoing. I wasn't as popular or confident as some of the other girls. I felt clumsy at times and had no idea how to be fashionable. I was a good student, but when it came to dating guys or asserting myself and saying *no* to friends, I caved in to peer pressure.

I just didn't know how to be myself completely, express my true desires, or say *no* to the things that didn't interest me. As I got older, I carried some of that self-doubt into my early adult years. The same cycle repeated itself at work, with friends, and with the guys I dated—I found that I struggled to assert myself. It made me nervous saying an outright *no* to people, and that made me a people pleaser.

I was unhappy with always being obedient, yet I felt trapped in that cycle. There were times when things got really out of control and I would go into a deep state of anger, hurt, and resentment. It would've been easier if someone had taught me the importance of assertiveness, and I wish I had known more about the dark feminine energy much sooner.

If I knew then what I know now, I could've been happier and more fulfilled, and I would've said an assertive *no* more often. I also didn't know how to be flirty and fun, or just be comfortable in my own skin without being afraid of being rejected and misunderstood. This is why I did my best to fit in, to have some kind of "normal" social life.

In time, I discovered that many other women out there experienced the same kind of inertia that I did in social situations. My problem was similar to most other women. I was conflicted about asserting myself, and I was not aware of the true importance of a woman standing her ground in every conceivable way.

I discovered this when I started reading more books and articles about the emotional complexity that women experience at times, which prevents us from going after everything we desire. This inner conflict has a lot to do with the development of our identity which stems from our beliefs, our upbringing, and the ideas we formed from a young age about what it means to be an empowered woman.

These beliefs, thoughts, attitudes, and ideas about femininity become the social constructs that determine our choices, behavior, and expectations. It is human nature to feel conflicted when our thoughts, ideas, and reactions are not acceptable to everyone else. When it is associated with strong, compelling emotions that challenge these social constructs, it is also frowned upon by people who believe that we need to be more obedient as women.

Being obedient and more accommodating is often associated with our light feminine side. The darker feminine energy is usually associated with our rebellious side, the side of us that does not want to conform to everyone else's expectations. This is where assertiveness comes into play. However, women, in general, still struggle to assert themselves despite all the progress we've made over the centuries to empower women at home and in the workplace. It is still often misinterpreted as being aggressive or self-promoting.

I have now come to terms with this: While it is normal to desire acceptance, it should not come at the expense of expressing your views, at times assertively. I also know firsthand how unhealthy it is to care about the judgments of others. We can listen with an open mind without allowing judgments or harsh opinions to get the better of us. When we depend entirely on the opinions and approval of others to progress in life, we will be held back because no one is waking up every morning dedicated to our lives. Only you can do that.

Being able to stand your ground, and own your own space takes courage today, and it always did in the past for women who were more in touch with their dark feminine energy. Throughout history, women were regarded as being "passive by nature." The expectation was that women should play more nurturing and subservient roles to men.

Assertiveness was not regarded as an attractive feminine quality to possess. However, throughout history, there were always women who challenged the status quo and who stood out for breaking that stereotyped expectation—that women should serve the whims and fancies of their husbands rather than their desires.

Today, owning your own space as a woman is not regarded as controversial as it once was in the past. Women have come a long way with time. Assertiveness is regarded as an attractive quality to possess. It is not as frowned upon as it once was. However, it is still somewhat conflicting for women who are not yet in touch with their dark feminine energy.

The sooner women break through those socialized constructs, the sooner they can take full charge of their life and avoid conflicting emotions that keep them stuck in being obedient. Standing your ground means making your own choices on the strength of your convictions. It also means being totally in control of your life, and that includes being accountable for your choices.

Not being easily swayed by the opinions of others or their manipulative tactics is a sign of being in touch with your dark feminine energy. It is a sign of independence and empowerment, and it is a powerful femme fatale characteristic. Another aspect of human behavior that can bring us down is engaging in negative self-talk. Keep this in mind always: Every negative thought you have about yourself is not true. We all possess strengths and weaknesses—having a perceived flaw in character is not a life sentence of shame. You can move past anything that you set your mind on.

Here's the thing about entrapping yourself in negativity: It will keep you stuck in low self-esteem and low self-confidence. You don't have to own your weaknesses. Own your strengths instead and focus on your best qualities because once a negative thought gets hardwired in your subconscious mind, it will stay there until you change it. You would need to shift that stuck energy created by negative thoughts about yourself.

This is really what holds many women back from being amazing— the fear of not being good enough or smart enough is quite often associated with negative self-talk. This is what shuts many women down from realizing their greatest potential. It's also what keeps them playing small.

Women are also very sensitive about their image and how they compare to other women. That is also an unhealthy habit because every woman is unique and special in her own right. Comparing yourself to others will lead to more negative thoughts about yourself. It was Ralph Waldo Emmerson who correctly stated that envy is ignorance and imitation is suicide.

I know how frustrating it can be to ignore your inner voice of rebellion, especially when it is in your best interest to listen carefully to what your intuition is saying to you. Dark feminine energy is today widely associated with using the power of your mind to seek the best solutions for your highest growth.

That voice of rebellion is often wisdom in disguise, emanating from the dark feminine intuition. Once you understand the flow of this energy, you will be willing to embrace more of this powerful aspect of your feminine identity and the results will be less frustration, self-doubt, second-guessing, and, definitely, less negative self-talk. It occurs when you learn how to trust your intuition more and go with it.

Dark thoughts also come from your intuition, and it is also wisdom emanating from your higher self or soul self-guiding you to better choices. Here's how I came to terms with the wisdom of my dark femininity: I began my journey by doing some shadow work on myself.

Our shadow selves are a reflection of the dark feminine energy. Discovering my shadow self was an enlightening and mind-opening encounter. I was able to dive deeper into traits that I rejected and even felt ashamed of in the past. I felt ashamed of the deep resentment I felt toward myself. Releasing all of that pain put me in touch with my dark feminine energy. I realized that I was not to blame for everything that went wrong in my life.

I started to forgive myself, and I also finally learned the hard lessons that I ignored before. Putting healthy boundaries in place was the next important step for me. The best part was mastering the art of saying no more often. I also made myself a priority and set out to transform all areas of my life so that it reflected a more empowered version of who I was. That empowered version was the femme fatale woman that I truly am today.

My mind was weaker than it is now. It was in a state of an illusory tug-of-war taking place between the light and dark feminine energy. I muscled up and decided to test some of my beliefs and take a long look at my life to ascertain which beliefs were holding me back. For example, I realized that I wasted more time dating all the wrong men instead of focusing on what I truly wanted—success and independence.

I dropped the trait of falling in love with the idea of finding Mr. Right every time I was attracted to a man. When I released that, I felt a surge of new energy within me. I became excited about the prospect of discovering more of my own talents, and if I was attracted to a man, it was not going to top the agenda of my life. It would be part of an ongoing journey of also exploring who I was as a femme fatale woman while being in a relationship with someone else.

As you will discover, the powerful femme fatale energy is seductive, fun, and adventurous to explore in a relationship with your partner. Dark feminine qualities are also associated with persistence, resilience, defiance, sensuality, assertiveness, and rebellion.

When a woman is more in touch with her dark feminine energy, she will also be less bothered about the opinion of others, and more in touch with what she wants and desires. Letting the darkness out does not mean that we are bad as women. It is only a label that we attach to situations based on social constructs stemming from what we've been conditioned to accept as being either good or bad. Letting out your inner darkness to take a stand to improve yourself, test your limits, and assert your independence is nothing to be ashamed of.

It is empowering as much as expressing love is empowering. Being strong and vulnerable at the same time is a combination of both light and dark feminine energy. We need them both to feel whole and validated. Shutting out the light or the dark feminine energy will give rise to self-doubt and painful emotions.

For example, not being able to express love, empathy, and compassion is a limitation that can cause us emotional pain. Similarly, not being able to rebel and address those things which bring us unhappiness will also hurt us emotionally and, in some cases, even result in trauma.

Here's what I did to help me get in touch with my dark feminine side: I made a list of the foxy femmes fatales that I admired and decided to explore their traits. When I did this, I realized that I also possess those traits. I realized that what I admired in them was also present inside of me. I was just not confident enough to allow those darker traits to shine out as much as I allowed the light to shine out.

The foxy women I admired were completely themselves. They gave themselves permission to be unapologetically authentic. It then dawned on me that unless I learned how to properly harness and achieve a balance of both the light and dark feminine sides of my personality, I would remain stuck where I was.

Doing the shadow work helped me to get more deeply in touch with the traits that I rejected about myself in my past. It was the first step that I took to reach out to my inner femme fatale. The father of modern psychology, Carl Jung, first coined the concept of *the shadow self.*

This is the dark side of feminine energy or the repressed psyche that people keep hidden in the shadows of their subconscious mind because it makes them uncomfortable. The dark side is what we reject at a subconscious level because a lot of it goes against the social constructs we grew up embracing, like: "Be good, kind, nurturing, and avoid having tantrums or reacting in anger in private or public."

Some women have been blessed with an early education on how to be confident, strong, independent, and an overachiever. A lot of women still suffer from insecurity and fears based on the somewhat incorrect grooming we received on how women *should behave, must behave, and be* regardless of personal preference, accomplishments, and desires. The world is good as much as it is a wicked place.

If you're good all the time, you will attract people who will use that against you, to trick you, and manipulate you. Beyond that, there are more advantages associated with dark feminine energy.

This side of you will help you reach clarity about the things that are truly worthy of pursuing.

Being in touch with your femme fatale will heighten your sense of awareness, thus enabling you to establish clear boundaries for yourself. Determination is a dark feminine trait and once you allow yourself to be more independent, you will soon be achieving all your goals and dreams. You will learn how to be unapologetically assertive where your needs are concerned.

These are all the qualities of the modern-day femme fatale. These types of women are putting themselves first and getting the most out of life on their terms. The modern-day femme fatale is more about independence. It is not about chasing men to conquer and destroy them.

A real femme fatale does not regard her sexuality as a weapon to destroy those that she conquers in bed. Instead, she uses her sexuality to enjoy herself and feel sensual. It is not at all about conquering and destroying a man. Sexuality, to a femme fatale, is something to enjoy for herself. The modern-day femme fatale is too preoccupied with her life, dreams, and priorities to pay attention to the external chaos of being a codependent and needy woman who needs to make impressions on people—unless it is important to persuade them to give her what she wants.

In most cases, subtle manipulation tactics may work better, and it is always wise to use subtle manipulation to win people over, as you will learn more about in this book. A true femme fatale will know how to use subtle manipulation to win hearts and minds, and not to destroy people or exert any vindictive control over anyone.

Dark feminine energy is about embracing your strengths that will help you to set boundaries, achieve your goals, feel more confident, and be in full control of your life. There is nothing toxic about dark feminine energy. It is all about gaining independence and feeling strong and capable from within.

Striking that balance between embracing both the light and dark sides of your personality is key to maintaining a positively inspiring outlook on life. Just as you need love, empathy, and compassion to enjoy fulfilling relationships, you also need your intuition and strength to guide you appropriately to ensure that you're not becoming a pushover for others to walk all over you.

Dark feminine energy is good when you can draw the line with people who are taking advantage of you, using you, or manipulating you in ways that reflect narcissistic traits—when it's all about them and what they want in a relationship, friendship, or professional association.

It is also the side of you that is more seductive and wilier to ensure that you will not be defeated by an opponent who has made themselves known to you as an opponent. Having too much light will keep you stuck in being obedient and subservient to people who are insincere and want to take advantage of your good nature.

Setting clear boundaries and protecting your personal space from being manipulated and used is where your dark feminine energy comes into play. No one wants to live in pain. Too much light will keep you stuck in pain and suffering because you'll be at the mercy of others who will take advantage of all that light that you're emitting.

Your dark feminine energy will help keep out people who are not sincere or have good company. It will keep you grounded in what is important to you, and help you to be the best version of who you are—to get exactly what you desire in life.

I am going to show you how to manifest your dark feminine energy. All the information you need to step into your femme fatale traits and own them is in this book waiting to be discovered. If you struggled with asserting yourself or did not feel confident in the past, you will learn how to achieve this.

You will also learn how to enjoy your own seductive personality, and what it means to be a high-value woman—to gain the respect you deserve. Get ready to fully explore what it means to be a femme fatale woman and discover how the concept has evolved since it made its exaggerated debut in Hollywood movies.

SECRET #1

You'll Never Be a Femme Fatale If You Don't Understand This

Dark matter and dark energy are two things we measure in the Universe that are making things happen, and we have no idea what the cause is.

– Neil deGrasse Tyson

The term *femme fatale* is a French term that means "lethal woman" or "disastrous woman." It clearly fits the image of how femmes fatales are still depicted in movies—as dangerous, sexy women who conquer men by using manipulation and their sexual prowess. In the movies, a femme fatale is headstrong, but also ruthless, and, therefore, can be a destructive force. The fictional portrayal of a femme fatale woman really exists in relation to a man. However, keep in mind that it is a fictional character.

What is important is that you create your own definition of what it means to be a femme fatale. What kind of femme fatale appeals to you? Here's a clue: The closer you get to understanding your dark feminine energy, the clearer your own definition will become. The movie definition of a femme fatale is someone else's dramatized interpretation of a femme fatale. You can create your own dramatized version that suits you best.

Picking up from where we left off with our discussion of Carl Jung's concept of shadow work and how important it is to start integrating our repressed qualities into our life—to make peace with them and learn the gifts of those repressed qualities—the femme fatale image that you conjure up can emerge from those repressed dark qualities in the shadows of your psyche.

Today, the femme fatale woman is also depicted in Hollywood movies in another way—one that is more relatable to badass women who want to manifest a unique destiny for themselves. These femmes fatales are headstrong women, but they are not necessarily destructive. Femmes fatales can be a positive force in the Universe. The new femmes fatales portrayed by Hollywood are badass women who are in touch with their superpowers.

They are bold, sassy, and fully in control of their life. They put up a good fight when needed, and this is the draw card that attracts their ideal partner in their life. A lot of women tend to identify better with this femme fatale image—I know I do. A femme fatale can be a woman who knows what she wants in life and she's not afraid of going after it. These new Hollywood femme fatale characters also make great sacrifices for their own happiness and will walk away from any situation that makes them feel powerless.

Actress Halle Berry comes to mind immediately. She starred in powerful Hollywood roles like in the James Bond movie *Die Another Day* where she was a tough CIA agent. She also took on a powerful femme fatale role in her depiction of *Catwoman*. In real life, she is tough as nails and determined as they come. She is well known for roughing things out to manifest her stardom in Hollywood.

When she was still working odd jobs and down on luck, Halle stayed in a homeless shelter. During interviews, she maintained that she just did what she had to to get by and not compromise her goals (Griffiths, 2017). She stuck it out to manifest the Hollywood stardom that she was chasing.

So you see, a femme fatale can be a very determined character who is willing to do whatever it takes to achieve their dreams. Halle Berry was always powerful in her own right and a real head-turner from a young age. She was a professional model before taking up acting and made it as the first runner-up in the Miss USA pageant in 1986.

My idea of a modern-day femme fatale is a woman who knows her true worth. I see the modern femme fatale as a woman who won't settle for anything that undermines her confidence or belittles her value. She knows that she deserves the best that life can offer. The femme fatale that I relate well to is a woman who is not needy, or clingy in her relationships with men.

A true femme fatale according to my standards—which identifies strongly with many of the modern, more grounded versions of Hollywood femme fatales today—is a strong, independent woman who puts up a good fight when her personal space is invaded by negativity or toxic people. She doesn't take kindly to being manipulated or controlled by anyone. She feels powerful in her unique way.

Her confidence, independence, intelligence, and the manner in which she can command her way in life, are a manifestation of her dark feminine energy. Such a woman is not interested in the opinions of others, nor does she care about being acceptable and pleasing. She can easily be her own raw, powerful, and mysterious self.

She is just not afraid to spread her kind of magic, which is a masterful combination of both light and dark energy. A femme fatale should be guided by a higher intuition that surpasses that of people-pleasing behavior—in other words, she always makes up her mind. She is bold and will strike out at anyone who gets under her skin or rubs her the wrong way. She is very much in touch with her dark feminine power and will use it accordingly to get her way.

After all, life is too short to waste any energy on things that are of little interest to you. Why be a people pleaser when you have superpowers to put to good use? A femme fatale should protect her personal space and value her time.

From personal experience, I do know this as a fact: When your light shines too brightly and you're always kind and soft with people, the negative ones will walk all over you. However, when you assert yourself and tell people in no uncertain terms that they've crossed a line with you, they will back off. A femme fatale knows how to be wily and she's decisive when she acts strongly and assertively against those she knows will not bring any good or meaningful energy to her life.

There are times when she will use her charms to win people's hearts and minds, and this kind of manipulative behavior is not vindictive on her part. It is a positive way of reinforcing her likability with others. A true femme fatale will not let anyone into her life who is going to stand in the way of her personal happiness. That's how deserving she feels of happiness, love, and success.

Her ability to overpower people who are not her friends (those who envy her or colleagues who are spiteful) is only to disarm them, and to ensure that they do not succeed with their hidden agendas. Femme fatale women are smart, crafty, and on top of their game in life, which is to *never be conquered or defeated*. Failure is not an option, nor is losing or giving up on her dreams.

She believes in fair play and winning, not just using her good looks and charm, but also the strength of her mind and by relying on her dark feminine energy to outshine those who wish to defeat her.

The world can be a wicked place as much as it is beautiful. Playing to win is always the best option to go with.

A true femme fatale recognizes the danger and the pleasure that life offers, and she is ready to outshine anyone who presents any kind of danger or threat to her happiness and peace of mind. A femme fatale is a woman who feels deserving of the attention of others. She is not interested in playing small, nor does she play big to get noticed. She plays the game of life according to her own rules, by pleasing the nature of her inner callings.

This is the spiritual aspect of the dark feminine energy. A femme fatale woman knows that she is extraordinary and unique, so she does not waste her time competing with other women. Her winning ways, talents, and determination to succeed are what sets her apart from others.

Mediocrity is not the way a femme fatale lives her life. She has extraordinary goals and is always pursuing her passions and interests. Her sense of adventure, play, and success is more important to her than being liked because she's acceptably angelic and pleasing. Her best qualities aim to make a positive impression on others because she is exquisitely proud of her own presence in the world. Just to strengthen your understanding of the femme fatale archetype, we will examine the origins of the femme fatale woman.

Origins of Dark Feminine Energy

History reveals many women who have embraced their dark feminine power. Some of these women continue to intrigue. That is because there is still a strong sense of resonance with how dark feminine energy was always frowned upon as being connected to evil. Women who were rebellious and different were called witches, especially if they displayed darker qualities. To this day, a woman who is in touch with her own darkness is feared. She is a threat to the meek and powerless. They do not connect to her darkness and refuse to acknowledge her light.

A woman who is in touch with her dark feminine side is often misunderstood. That is because there is nothing fragile about empowerment. Some of the ancient mythological goddesses are still revered today for the darkness they displayed. Even during ancient times, women who were regarded as goddesses were worshiped because they were manifesting their darker feminine qualities. Here are two well-known goddesses who are still worshiped today for the embodiment of their own darkness.

Kali

She is a Hindu goddess who possesses two faces and may look scary to an unsuspecting observer. However, her power of destruction is largely received as being very healing to those who receive her strength. Hindu worshipers turn to Kali to overcome their fears and to gain the courage they need to transcend challenges and accomplish great things. Kali gives them confidence. She has a wild look, yet she is also regarded as a divine mother to her followers.

Her believers see her as a protective deity who is also a source of blessings. She is known as the goddess of destruction and time, and she is by nature wild, untamed, primal, and powerful in her desire to conquer anyone standing in her way. Around her neck, there are skulls that symbolize liberation and the need to destroy false beliefs of the mind—that are not serving you for your highest good.

Kali also has special powers. She possesses psychic gifts that can remove any karma around a person who is a believer. The severed head that she carries with her represents the ego or false self, and the nakedness reflects the need for authenticity. Westerners are often alarmed by the raw dark energy of Kali.

However, she is a rebel, like all women who embrace their own darkness. Kali appears to be always ready to rise to power and take charge of any situation. Hindus believe that when you channel energy, you will be able to connect to her wildness and destroy old constructs in your life that are no longer serving you.

If you don't even believe in her, her symbolic nature is evidence of an ancient belief in the power of dark feminine energy. There is nothing tame about it at all. It is destructive as much as it is creative. It has been believed since ancient times that the dark feminine energy will also bring out the inner warrior in you, especially when the need arises to assert and fight valiantly for yourself.

The consciousness of Kali's symbolic power of dark feminine energy can help you create a new destiny for yourself. Her destructive nature calls forth a new path for those who yearn for transformation in their life (Gurukul, n.d.). As you contemplate Kali's destructive nature, call forth a new destiny for yourself. Think about what you would love to destroy in your life and as you destroy the old, get ready to embrace a new vision for your life.

By harnessing the magic of the dark feminine energy, you can get rid of your old constructs and bring about the change you desire from within. Make a list of things in your life that appear not to be going your way. For example, are you unhappy in your current relationship or job? Do you feel like you're living someone else's life and not doing enough to explore what you really want in life?

Examine each area of your life and closely examine everything that's going on for you. Ask yourself what you would love to change about your life, and plot a way forward to create the desired change, one step at a time.

Lilith

Lilith is a figure found in Judeo-Christian and Mesopotamian mythology. She is largely portrayed as a demon seductress for her independent ideas and rebellious nature. According to the myth, Lilith was the first wife of Adam. She was, therefore, the first woman on the planet who refused to be subjugated by the patriarchal nature of man. She refused to submit to her husband's authority and quite rightfully emerged as a woman of strength, independence, and warrior-like qualities.

It is this quality that has set her up in history as a demon woman who is in touch with her dark feminine side. It is this rebellious side of our feminine nature that is associated with dark feminine energy. The darker traits of assertiveness, destruction, power, rebelliousness, seduction, and personal autonomy are attractive to men who value strong and fiery women.

Men too have a dark side to them and they also use this energy to assert their authority and protect their interests. The dark feminine energy is, therefore, not a curse at all, but a gift that can be used for manifestation, protection, seduction, and enjoyment. It's the side of you that balances the light, that frees up your perspective so that you don't end up being stuck in social constructs of how women must or should be.

A woman can be dark and light in her relationship with her partner, as long as the relationship itself is of high quality, empowering, and overall satisfying to be in. Allow Lilith's freedom to inspire you to change things in your life that may be stifling you right now.

The light and shadow sides of Lilith reflect her need for freedom. Be open and willing to express your needs to your partner. Reflect on the kind of freedom you would love to enjoy in your relationships with others. Always remember that a femme fatale woman defines what makes her happy in life, and that includes the kind of relationships she wishes to explore with others.

If you are in a relationship or friendship that feels burdensome, restrictive, and manipulative, then start examining your options to either express your needs to your partner or friend or to limit the amount of time you spend with them. You might also want to examine your options to completely exit toxic relationships. Free yourself from situations that are toxic and manipulative by nature.

Why Does Dark Feminine Energy Matter?

Over the centuries, women have been wired or programmed to be more ladylike, to conform to the expectations of men, to be nurturers, and carers, and to be more angelic as opposed to being devilish or rebellious. It is important to point out here that we've also created labels to describe human behavior as being either *good* or *bad*. From a spiritual perspective, everything is in balance and as it should be.

In other words, self-expression as a reflection of who you are is neither good nor bad. Everything is as we perceive it and how we behave. Whether in a combination of dark or light, this helps us get what we want in life. Our actions should, therefore, be more supportive of our plans. If assertiveness is required, then don't hold back and make it a shadow.

Embrace it and use this strong trait that you possess to empower yourself. If distancing yourself, from things, places, and people that upset you, feels right, then do exactly that—even if it may seem like a harsh choice to others. Exaggerating or denying the light and darkness in you will feel repressive and will frustrate you. It is always better to let people know when they've overstepped their mark with you. It neutralizes strong emotions immediately. Finding the right balance between your light and dark sides is important. The challenge is to make peace with the presence of both light and darkness in you.

Repression will lead to more frustration and unnecessary feelings of guilt and shame. When you are at peace with your darkness and light and find a healthy balance to manifest your desires, you will have more peace in your life. You will also experience less stress. Embracing the dark feminine in you will also decrease the pressure you put on yourself when you judge yourself too harshly. Here are more reasons to explore when considering the benefits of getting in touch with your dark energy (Jaye, 2022):

1. It will help you to let go of things more easily with lesser guilt or shame.

2. You can connect more with your inner strength.

3. You will feel more comfortable with yourself and less conflicted.

4. You will feel more comfortable in your own body and sexuality.

5. You will feel more creative, especially when you get rid of the things that are not working in your life, without feeling guilty about doing so.

6. You will be more accountable and less of a victim of things happening to you. Assertiveness, saying no, and holding yourself accountable for your choices puts you in full control of your choices.

How to Manifest Your Inner Femme Fatale

Now that you know what makes a femme fatale powerful in her own right, you too can start manifesting your inner dark feminine energy. At the core of manifesting your inner femme fatale is the grounding belief that you are worthy of living your best life. Femmes fatales always feel worthy of getting the most joy out of life—on their terms. When we begin the practice of manifesting anything we desire, it is always important to identify problems or things that appear to be causing a certain degree of discomfort, distress, or unhappiness.

Once you've identified your pain points, you must take a look at what you are currently doing that is not giving you the results you want. The goal of manifesting your inner femme fatale is to become a stronger and more empowered version of yourself—to ultimately live a life that feels right for you.

It requires that you take a deeper look at areas in your life that do not reflect everything that you want to experience. By manifesting your inner femme fatale, you will be taking full control of those situations to bring about a balance of dark and light feminine energy. This will ensure that you correctly project your needs and go after your goals.

Manifesting your inner femme fatale aims at replacing too much light feminine energy with a balance of both dark and light energy. It is this balance that will restore a more equitable outcome in all situations, one that does not leave you feeling unhappy or always wanting more. You must aim to feel satisfied that you are on track to achieving your goals in all areas of your life, and that the journey is not frustrating you altogether.

If you desire a more equitable relationship with your partner and are currently unhappy with the distribution of power in your relationship, then it may be a pain point that requires a more balanced approach to reaching a more equitable outcome. For example, if you are emanating too much light energy, your partner could be taking you for granted right now in your relationship.

When you shift your behavior to accommodate more of your dark feminine side by asserting your needs and not always bending to please them, you will be bringing in the dark feminine energy. The first part of this manifestation exercise is to help you to get fully in touch with your inner femme fatale traits.

The second part is to help you to identify areas in your life that require transformation. By harnessing the dark feminine energy, you can bring about a balance to restore feeling more satisfied with your choices. Here are some steps to take to begin manifesting your inner femme fatale.

Make a List

Identify the femme fatale women you admire, whether they are celebrities or women that you know personally and admire. They could also be figures from history or spiritual traditions that resonate with you.

List the Traits You Admire About Them

For example, it might be that they are fit and strong physically, or their assertiveness and ability to express themselves clearly may be something you admire and wish to manifest more of in your life.

Ask Yourself

Why do you admire those traits, and how would you love to manifest those traits in specific areas in your life?

Examine Your Current Mindset

Identify why these traits are lacking in you, or why you may be suppressing those traits right now. You might be surprised to learn that you do possess those traits but may be suppressing them for reasons linked to a limiting belief or a socialized construct. How does it make you feel, knowing that you are not living up to your greatest potential?

Investigate Limitations

Give yourself some space to explore how limiting beliefs have held you back in the past. For example, not being assertive may be keeping you stuck in relationships with people who are using you or taking advantage of you. You may be putting up with their manipulation to avoid a confrontation because you are not confident enough to express your needs. This cycle may be constantly repeating itself. It is what happens when you are only manifesting your light feminine side. People by nature will take advantage of you.

Commit to Succeed

Once you've identified those areas in your life where manifestation can heal and transform your life, commit to bringing about the necessary behavioral changes to support your goals. For example, if someone is taking advantage of you at work or in your personal relationships, then you need to start asserting yourself more often and learn how to say no more often without being apologetic about it. When you say, "No more," often, you are also giving yourself permission to invest your energy in manifesting what you truly desire, and less of what others expect of you.

Have a Clear Vision

When you have a clear vision of the change you want to manifest, always keep the end goal in mind. Not having a clear vision of your goal will hinder your success. Just as world athletes are constantly focused on the end goal of winning, you need to always be consistent with your end vision in mind when manifesting change.

Rewire Your Brain

Using visualization to remind yourself of your goals will also rewire your subconscious mind and your thinking patterns. This is how you will be able to shift your behavior to match the new, empowered vision of yourself. Always remember that repetition is important to hardwire new habits. Meditating on your vision of the newly empowered femme fatale version of yourself is, therefore, part of the process of reconditioning your thinking and behavioral patterns.

Focus on the End Result

If you see yourself traveling around the world in your vision and being your own empowered boss, then you must be clear about changing your current work situation to accommodate your goal. In your vision, give more detail on how you will go about transforming your life. You might want to visualize the steps that you would need to take to make the required adjustment from being employed to becoming your own boss. The more detail you give to your vision, the clearer and more tangible it will become.

Pay Attention to the Frequency of Your Thoughts and Feelings

Finally, during the manifestation process, you will need to take cognizance of how frequencies work and how you can adjust your frequency to bring about the desired results. How you think and feel about the goals that you are manifesting is a very important part of the manifestation process.

Adopt an Attitude of Gratitude

Be thankful every day for the little blessings in your life. Counting your blessings daily has a great impact on the brain. It reduces stress, grounds you in your present reality, and increases positive feelings (Chowdhury, 2019). A positive vibe that is entrenched in deep feelings of gratitude will make all things more joyful and the process of manifestation deeply rewarding.

For example, when things don't work out exactly as you want them to, instead of focusing on the perceived drawbacks and getting stuck in negative emotions, count your blessings. Also, look for hidden blessings in all challenging situations. Ask yourself what you have learned in the process and how you can improve in your journey of manifesting your desires.

Be thankful for the things that are going your way. Failure is only a label that we attach to situations when we give up on the things that matter to us. Be thankful when you fail for the lessons and insight that you've gained. Always remember that a femme fatale is much craftier than just sitting back and accepting temporary setbacks. A true femme fatale thrives when she's challenged because she can put her thinking cap on to find inspiring and creative solutions.

Understanding the Law of Vibration for Manifestation

Understanding the law of vibration as it is widely known lies at the heart of understanding how frequencies work for manifestation purposes. According to this law, you must invoke the vibration or feeling of what you desire from within yourself. When you start emitting positive feelings about the things that you want to manifest, you will enjoy great results and much sooner than you thought was possible.

The law works like this: When you feel good about the changes you are making, your vibrational frequency will improve and increase. This will, in turn, allow you to attract more of what you desire. For example, if you feel good about protecting your space from toxic people and you've committed to eliminating negative people from your life, you will start vibrating at a higher frequency immediately. You will want to stay there and keep them out.

Think about a time in your life when you felt very anxious or irritable. You would know from experience what a damper those feelings can have on your mood throughout the day. It feels like a dark cloud is hanging over your head. You most likely know from experience how powerful it can be to shift your mood by thinking more positive thoughts or doing something to release you from the grip of anxiety or even mild depression.

Similarly, when you start feeling good about your goals, you will start manifesting them more clearly. It is all about tuning into a positive, more supporting frequency daily to support a more positive manifesting outcome.

Also, when you take daily action to ensure a positive mind frame, it will consistently raise your vibrational frequency. This, in turn, will bring about more success in your manifestation ability. Tuning into positive frequencies more often will also allow you to eliminate the things in your life that you no longer desire to experience.

The bottom line to manifesting change is being able to consistently tune into a positive frequency—you must feel good about what you are manifesting and believe in it. Meditation, visualization, using positive affirmations, and cutting out negative self-talk will raise your vibrational frequency. Self-care is also a powerful way of raising your vibrational frequency. We will discuss more of this in the next chapter.

CLOSING AFFIRMATION:

My authenticity is my power!

SECRET #2

Powerful Manifestation Methods Charged by Dark Feminine Energy

What you think, you become.
What you feel, you attract.
What you imagine, you create.

–Buddha

How to Use Dark Feminine Energy to Ignite Your Manifesting

Manifestation is grounded in your thoughts, action, and beliefs. One of the Universal laws known as the *law of attraction* is also based on the principle that you are the creator of your destiny—what you think about you will attract more of. So, if your thoughts and actions are more fear-based as a result of poor self-confidence and low self-esteem, then you will not attract the desired results in your life.

Manifesting your dark feminine energy is going to help you overcome those limitations. A true femme fatale is a determined and confident woman who does not compare her talents with anyone else. Instead, she uses self-doubt to examine areas in her life to determine where improvement is needed.

So, if you're feeling insecure because you may not be as skilled as others in your field of interest or living the life you desire to live right now, then one way of achieving your goals would be to learn more from others in your manifestation journey.

For example, if you are fearful of public speaking but recognize the need to do more of it as it will enhance your professional brand or uplift your self-image, then that is the first step toward achieving personal empowerment in the space of public speaking. The next step would be to master the art of effective public speaking by learning from professionals who are doing well in this space.

Once you've learned the basics of how to overcome stage fright and be an effective public speaker, you would need to practice more and sign up for events that can open up opportunities for you to put your skills to good use. This is how you can empower yourself in areas that are of interest to you: decide, commit, and take the necessary steps that will guarantee your success.

When you are intentional about your purpose and mission in life, your chances of success increase. Oprah Winfrey, one of America's top TV hosts, is famous for always reiterating her own femme fatale philosophy which is: Take control of your life, make your own choices, and live your dreams. Oprah, like so many other successful and empowered women, understands the value of going all out to realize a dream.

According to her, it's not only about focusing on the success that you're seeking but on the significance of your entire journey (Quora, 2011). The quality of that journey is also important—all outcomes are dependent on the choices that you make.

Realizing the dream is therefore also about taking small steps and celebrating the victory of those small steps because they all add up! All steps make up the entire journey that you're on right now. Embrace the beauty of every moment and the magic of taking small steps.

The journey to true empowerment is also about becoming fully present in every moment of your life—to decide how it's going to be for you. A true femme fatale is not someone who sits idly by and accepts what comes her way. A true femme fatale is someone who has a say in her own choices and she enjoys every small step that she is taking to build the life of her dreams.

If that small step includes taking more lessons to perfect her public speaking skills because she sees it as a long-term career investment, then that is exactly where she will devote her energy as her long-term success will depend on possessing effective public speaking skills. It is a question of prioritizing activities that are aligned with the goals that you've set for yourself.

Oprah's philosophy also sums up what the law of attraction is all about. Just thinking about what you want will not make them magically appear in your life and will not result in powerful manifestation. You have to meet your intentional thoughts with purposeful and powerful actions to achieve the desired results.

It is the dark feminine energy or femme fatale traits of resilience, determination, and selfish motivation that will keep you on track with the things that are important to you. Being selfish in the pursuit of your goals is a virtue and not something to be ashamed of.

A femme fatale loves herself unconditionally because she is no longer labeling what is good or bad. She is instead going with her own natural flow and inner wisdom to find true fulfillment for herself. That requires a commitment to embrace the duality of the nature of her existence—being willing to step into the zone of trusting her instinct to manifest what she wants using her dark feminine energy.

A femme fatale knows that her light side will always keep her grounded in knowing how to achieve a healthy balance of being a humanitarian without compromising on her need to manifest a life worthy of living according to her standards. As long as you are not being destructive in your path to success by belittling others or pushing them down to get to the top, there is nothing unhealthy about choosing your goals as a priority over the judgmental or negative opinions of others.

History has shown us that women who refused to surrender their dreams when they came under any kind of external pressure achieved greatness and success, far beyond their initial expectations. They were determined and not afraid to empower themselves in their fields of interest. Not only did these women achieve their goals, but they also reshaped history and society's limited views about the potential of women.

For example, Florence Nightingale was a devoted Christian woman, but she was also in touch with her dark feminine energy and defied her family, friends, and society when she refused to settle for marriage. She chose to become a nurse to care for the sick and injured soldiers, instead of succumbing to a predestined future based on her family's and larger societal expectations.

Florence believed that it was her *highest calling* to be of value to others by serving injured and sick soldiers. She was born into a very wealthy family, and there was no need for her to work a day in her life. However, it was her goal to become a nurse. She wanted to follow her inner calling and explore her talents this way. So, she went ahead and received the training that was required to become a nurse in 1844, after finally obtaining permission to do so from her very wealthy and reluctant father. Today, history remembers her as the founder of modern nursing (The National Archives, n.d.).

The key is believing that it is within your power to achieve your goals and taking meaningful action to ensure your success. As you begin your journey of manifestation, always remember that the real destination is the actual journey, the growth encounter is where empowerment happens.

Achieving your goals must feel like it is going to be the most natural consequence of the action that you are taking every step of the way of manifesting them. As you start activating the dark feminine energy from within, you will also synchronously start attracting people, places, and things in your life that will support your journey and your progress. This happens mysteriously but also intentionally.

This is what synchronicity is all about. It is about manifesting having an effect on what is happening in our external world by manipulating our thoughts and beliefs to support what we desire to have in life. Synchronicity occurs when what is happening in your external world matches what is happening in your internal world. It is the power of the mind that is connecting to the external world and attracting all the wonderful coincidences we encounter that supports our manifestation process.

For example, when you are confident and perfectly in tune with your vision, you will start attracting opportunities and people in your life that support your goals. Synchronicity is the ability of our mind to connect to others, events, and opportunities through space and time. From a spiritual perspective, it is the Universal law of attraction at play. This is why it is so important to get rid of the weeds of negativity in your mind, and plant, instead, the seeds of inspiration (Richardson, 2022).

Scripting the Life of Your Dreams

One way of becoming very clear about your goals is to begin the journey of scripting. Think of this as the process of determining what you want and how you will go about getting it. It often happens that because we have so many things going on in our current reality, we keep pushing aside the things that are most meaningful for us to achieve in life. You may have a lot of things going on in your mind right now.

Also, stress can make us have the most far-fetched fantasies that are also not properly aligned with our goals and dreams. These fantasies can be a cause of conflict when they seem more desirable than reality. It is the real goals that you set for yourself that will bring you great fulfillment if you achieve them. Leave out the fantasies and use visualization instead to imagine achieving all of your goals.

Everything becomes attainable when you have a plan in place. Even the Eiffel Tower needed to have a plan in place before it could be built. For example, instead of fantasizing about finding the perfect rich man of your dreams to fulfill your financial and relationship needs, try setting more realistic goals for yourself that will see you attract more money for yourself. Make a list of how much you would realistically like to earn in the next 12 months and create a plan of action to reach that revenue target.

Similarly, make a bucket list of all the great adventures you want to experience, and then create a plan of action that you can implement to achieve those goals. Your first task would be to start a journal and divide it into sections for each area of your life: vocational, educational, love, relationships, family, spiritual, financial, and recreational.

Write down how it is at present and next to each reality write down a goal that you want to accomplish with a timeline in place for each and every goal that you wish to achieve in all areas of your life. Without creating timelines, your goals will remain an *out-of-reach fantasy,* which will only make you more unhappy with your current reality.

Also, creating a timeline for each goal will make things clearer and it will begin to feel well within your reach to accomplish as opposed to writing down goals without chunking them down into bite-sized more-manageable targets to achieve. Once again, embrace the magic of small steps when creating timelines for each goal that you write down in every area of your life. So, for each area of your life, start scripting what you would love to achieve and begin taking meaningful steps toward the realization of those goals.

Instead of going into a fantasy mode, stick with goals that feel right for you from within. If something feels right and it is coming from a deep desire or need, then your chances of achieving those goals will be much higher. The more you believe in your dreams and goals, the greater the magic will be as you also surrender them lovingly to the Universe.

When you become very clear about what you want, then your communication with the Universe also gets clearer, and this will activate the law of attraction to work in your favor. Remember that you are always getting what you want, but when you're clear and have eliminated the doubts, fantasies, and fragmented ideas of what you want, it will make a big difference in the manifestation process. Your energy will shift accordingly—to focus more on those things that you want and have a firm intention of achieving.

Manifestation will also become more focused and powerful. This is another way that dark feminine energy serves you. When you are busy conforming to socialized constructs instead of going after what you want, the Universe responds accordingly. Conversely, when you do not live in fear of being judged, rejected, or misunderstood and just go after your desires, you will attract everything that you need, and your life will feel more authentic, whole, and meaningful.

Your dark feminine energy reflects the side of you that is unapologetic about fulfilling your needs as a more urgent priority rather than conforming to the whims and ideas of others. A true femme fatale knows that everyone is living according to their own standards, so she has to also uplift her life according to her standards, rules, and norms.

Make it a priority to script the life of your dreams clearly, creatively, and in a way that feels right for you. Put in as much detail as possible and remind yourself of your goals daily. Be very focused, purposeful, and inspired from within to manifest magnificent results and all will fall into place. Also, be willing to make adjustments as you progress and expand on those initial ideas that support the realization of your goals.

You can also create a vision board, which is very popular for enhancing the scripting process. Scripting your life's goals using a vision board is a wonderful way of creating a roadmap for the life that is most appealing to you. It will help you feel like everything that you desire is within your reach.

No one should be in a position of just getting by in life: Accepting a reality that does not meet your expectations is a rather dull and uninspiring way to live. Life is full of wonder, possibility, and passion when you allow it to be that way—when you stop resisting those qualities within yourself, your inner femme fatale will emerge. Have a plan and go for it!

Allow your determined, charismatic inner femme fatale to emerge every day so that you can say no more often to those things that do not matter, and say YES to those things that do matter. You can have your dream life as long as you believe in it and are willing to put some skin in the game—meaning that you will do whatever it takes to make things happen!

Using the Power of Visualization to Manifest Your Goals

Visualization is how we get by every day of our life—so you are already familiar with how to visualize the outcome you desire. You are already using visualization in your life, whether you're aware of it or not. For example, when we need someone else's approval for something to go ahead with our plans (like a professional colleague or a partner), we tend to go over our approach in our minds. This involves some type of visualization.

Also, when we know who we need to approach for their approval, we can anticipate potential setbacks. This will help you to strategize accordingly to ensure a positive outcome. As children, we also visualized the things that we wanted and needed. Most children do that before they get their way with their parents. They also pretend that they already have what they want, like a pet or a favorite game. This is what visualization is all about, *imagining that what we want is what we already have!*

As much as scripting is an important part of the manifestation process, so is visualization. Once you're clear about the path you will follow, you need to visualize that you have it already and use your imagination to pretend that you are already living the life that you desire. For example, if you always wanted to produce your own documentary on a subject of interest, then the more time you spend visualizing it as if it already happened, the greater your chances are of manifesting it.

Think of visualization as if you're playing a game of pretend. However, you must visualize it and feel like you've already manifested the things that you desire. Plus, having a plan of action in place to support the manifestation of your goals will guarantee your success. The formula for manifesting is, therefore: Scripting, visualization, and taking daily purposeful action to realize the full vision you have for your life.

What we think about and visualize is truly what we bring about. Whether you're spiritual or not doesn't really matter when it comes to manifestation, and using visualization is an important tool to achieve it. The Universe will support you to attract everything that you want, it always does because that is the nature of the law of attraction.

Visualization also helps us to imprint everything that is important to us in our subconscious mind. When your goals and visualization of achieving those goals become hardwired in your brain, it will also become second nature to you to act accordingly to bring about its manifestation.

Think of visualization as the process of creating a new "mental habit" to guarantee your ongoing success. Visualization is not a mystical thing that will magically bring you what you want—instead, it is a process that is very much grounded in neuroscience.

Visualization is known to increase memory retention, improve performance, and increase creativity. When we take time out daily to visualize our long- and short-term goals, we are being creative and we are learning how to better use our brains to help us succeed.

Here's how visualization helps your brain to function optimally: It strengthens neural connections in the prefrontal cortex of the brain. This part of the brain is also known as the executive center. It is where all decision-making, planning, and execution of tasks take place. When you are creating pictures in your mind of the changes that you want to implement in every area of your life through scripting and visualization, you are also helping the executive center of your brain to direct new behavior, actions, and thoughts to remind you of your goals.

When new thoughts, ideas, and behavior become hardwired in the prefrontal cortex of the brain, moving toward the achievement of your goals will feel like second nature to you (Self Help Motivation, 2021).

The more you visualize what you want in life and feel connected to those goals, the more positive you will also feel about their attainment. Your mind will believe that it is happening right now, and this will increase feelings of confidence and positivity. This is why it is also important to celebrate the milestones along the way of your journey and count your blessings more often.

You will feel good about your achievements, and that reinforces more positive behavior to continuously support your manifestation journey. You can visualize your future and the manifestation of more femme fatale qualities that are vital to your ongoing journey. If you have always been more of a pushover, giving people the benefit of the doubt too often even when they didn't always deserve it, you can change that trait by visualizing a more assertive version of yourself.

It is not necessary to always give people all your attention. Femmes fatales prefer to moderate their behavior, especially when it comes to always pleasing others or being good all the time. Here's a very simple way to help you with visualization (Self Help Motivation, 2021).

1. Take at least 20 min to meditate daily and visualize the things that are important to you. Remember that you can use this same process to objectively observe challenges and problems that you need to resolve.

2. Decide what your goal is, or decide on what is creating discomfort in your life that requires a resolution.

3. Find a comfortable spot, somewhere you feel in the zone. It could be out in nature, where you feel relaxed, or even at your office desk because it's convenient to do this for 20 min before you begin your day at work. The more private the space you use for visualization, the better—it is a personal exercise, so keep it private. Make it your special time!

4. Picture yourself doing whatever action is necessary to reach your goal, or allow your brain to search for solutions to the

current challenges you are facing. For example, you can visualize your entire day in advance, and all the activities that you must attend to which will take you closer to the realization of your short-, medium-, and long-term goals.

5. If you are focusing on an ongoing problem or challenge, then visualize the desired outcome that feels right for you, as if it has already happened.

6. Imagine how wonderful it feels to have everything that you desire right now and feel worthy of it manifesting in your life as if it is already yours.

7. Once you've completed the visualization process, implement the action that you need to take to manifest your goals. For example, if you've visualized that you are healthy, sporty, and following an inspiring self-care plan that keeps you consistently healthy, then follow through with that vision by doing those things.

Meditations for Manifesting

Meditation is a very profound way of connecting with your desires and goals. Not only is it relaxing and soothing for the body, mind, and spirit, but most guided meditations (which are a great way to start manifesting with meditation) are designed in a way to uplift and motivate you toward the attainment of your goals. Meditation for manifesting also allows you to cultivate an attitude of peace and abundance at the same time. Inner peace is key to manifesting because a turbulent mind often misdirects energy and does not align well with feelings of positivity.

Using meditation as a daily powerful visualization exercise will continuously keep you centered, focused, and inspired every day. It will also make it easier to ward off negativity in your life. Manifestation meditations have been designed to assist you to become more of a success magnet and less of a worrier. When you give more energy to manifesting the life you desire and less energy to fearful thoughts, it is only a question of time before you reap the full results of your daily meditation goals.

All you need is to dedicate at least 20 min of your day to meditate on any area of your life that requires more energy. For example, if you feel fearful and are stuck in limiting thoughts and beliefs about money, yet you desire to have more money, then abundance meditations will work well to shift your mindset from being fearful about money to feeling more abundant about money and acquiring the things that you need in your life.

A great meditation for attracting abundance and reflecting on your attitude to money is the *Ho'oponopono* meditation for money and abundance. It is based on an ancient Hawaiian prayer and has been adopted to attract abundance and develop a higher awareness of money. It is also a gratitude prayer. As you've already learned in the previous chapter, adopting an attitude of gratitude will make you feel more positive. You can find Ho'oponopono meditations on YouTube for money, abundance, and forgiveness.

Self-forgiveness is also a wonderful way of releasing emotional baggage from the past. Forgiving yourself for past mistakes is an important way of practicing self-love. It will also help you to release feelings of guilt for not putting yourself first in the past, especially if you were always more giving to others to conform to their needs and expectations.

When your mind supports more abundant thoughts and feelings, then undoubtedly you will also start getting more creative with how you attract money and abundance into your life. You can pause here to go online right now and check out some powerful meditations available on YouTube. There are lots of other guided manifesting meditations to help you manifest your desires accordingly.

Try starting your day off first thing in the morning with a manifesting meditation for abundance, love, or attracting more positive energy in your life. Remember whenever you feel a lack in yourself, your abilities, or your confidence, then it is time to start doing more manifesting meditations to rectify those negative feelings (Keithley, 2022).

The Power of Music

Dancing is a wonderful way of getting in touch with your dark feminine energy. Let music be the food of love and inspiration and release your inhibitions by embracing dance as a powerful way of transforming body, mind, and spirit. Dancing also brings us more in touch with our physical existence and it's a wonderful way of letting go. Using music combined with dance (or even on its own) has a way of getting us out of our heads. This is why workout classes combine exercise with high-energy music. It helps to release excess energy from your body and negative emotions.

So, put on your dancing shoes and sign up for a dark-energy feminine dance class. Belly dancing or Latin-American dance routines are invigorating, fun, and a niche to explore, but any dance workout like Zumba or African dance classes will also help manifest more of your dark feminine energy. You will learn more about dance forms, be introduced to pulsating, hypnotic, and exotic music, and you will establish a wonderful outlet for your dark feminine energy. Free expression, sensuality, and confidence are dark feminine traits. Dance and the power of music will get you closer to these traits. It is an incredibly liberating and joyous way of shifting your energy!

Being Aware of the Phases of the Moon

The moon has more control over our thoughts and emotions than the sun does. Whether you're into astrology or not, becoming aware of the phases of the moon and its impact on our moods, thoughts, and feelings will put you more in touch with yours. Each phase of the moon represents a different stage of the moon's movement around the Earth.

When we connect more to the four phases, we can also use them as a way of assessing our manifesting progress. The moon is also associated with a woman's intuition and unconventional ideas. Paying attention to the phase of the moon and manifesting more of your inner dark feminine energy will help you to become more authentic and less influenced by the opinion of others.

I personally love observing the moon at night. I make it a point to get more in touch with myself during all four phases of the moon. Paying attention to the moon phases helps me to identify where I am in my life. Getting excited about meditating with moon meditations is something that you should be doing too. Moon meditations are a wonderful way of preparing yourself to enter new phases in your life. Every cycle of the moon's orbit should be regarded as a new phase.

Connecting with the power of a full moon or a blood moon is an excellent time to decide on the major things happening in your life. Think about the things that you need to let go of or do to bring about greater manifestations. In ancient times, a full moon was considered the best witching time to make powerful spells. In modern times, spells are used to manifest what we desire.

There is a beautiful energy about a full moon when it lights up the sky. It beautifies the darkness around us. In the same way, use it to manifest more dark feminine energy in your life and come up with unique solutions for your ongoing challenges. Allow your intuition to guide you during every phase of the moon.

Celebrate a full moon as the end of a negative or stressful cycle and vow to make some inspiring changes in its place. Every lunar cycle is special and, therefore, every moon phase comes with a special message and meaning. A waning moon reminds me to rest, recharge and relook at my goals to determine if there are changes I need to consider. A waning moon is reminding us all of the importance of getting enough rest in between manifesting and letting go. Here's how each phase of the moon can assist you in manifesting your dark feminine side (Nast, 2022).

1. **New moon:** Go over your goals, adjust them, and make new ones each month to change anything about your life, choices, or relationships. Let the new moon put you in charge of your life by taking stock of where you are in your journey and what new, positively inspiring possibilities lie ahead of you. Life is a fluid process, so allow for adjustments and flexibility each month by assessing your goals, and your progress when a new moon shines its intuitive wisdom on you.

2. **Waxing crescent moon:** It occurs after the new moon, and looks like a silver crescent. Use this phase of the moon to decide how to manifest the new moon goals that you've set. Allow the waxing crescent moon to give you a boost of inspiration and a chance to reflect on your new moon goals.

3. **Waxing gibbous moon:** This phase of the moon signifies a time to surrender to yourself, to release yourself from any stress or negativity, and to withdraw to soften more toward yourself. Take stock of the things that are weighing you down, and commit to releasing yourself from them. Take a rest, enjoy a long swim, or spend some time meditating out in nature during this moon phase.

4. **Full moon:** A full moon is a powerful time in a lunar cycle. It signifies change, healing, and even celebration of where you are in your life. Always count your blessings when the full moon appears in the night sky. The moon is always supercharged when it's full. Do a sound meditation with powerful gongs and rejoice in your achievements.

Also, let go joyously of the things that are no longer serving you and remind yourself of your superpowers to achieve whatever you set your mind to. At every full moon, reconnect with your goals and recommit to everything that is important to you in your life.

CLOSING AFFIRMATION:

I powerfully connect to the vast and ever-expanding nature of the Universe to seek the abundance that I wish to attract in my life!

Channeling Your Dark Feminine Energy

No one can live their dream life without putting in some effort. This is why manifestation is a process. It is more complicated than you think. Manifesting is a journey of hard work, commitment, dedication, and self-belief. However, once you get the hang of it—manifesting your heart's desires will be fun and personally fulfilling. Arianna Huffington, author and cofounder of HuffPost, correctly stated that you have to keep doing what you dream of doing even while you're afraid (Hutto, n.d.).

Manifesting your dreams takes courage, commitment, and discipline. It is not an overnight journey, but it will build you for even greater things to come. When you put in the effort to achieve the results you want, moments become milestones to celebrate. It is a femme fatale quality to revel in those moments of self-achievement.

A true femme fatale also knows that she will be tested along the way. This is why she depends on her dark feminine energy and is not afraid of being crafty and manipulative to secure her own interests. You must, therefore, choose a path of love for yourself—when things get tough, doing what you love will always matter!

By committing to do the things that you love and manifesting what is most dear to you, you are securing a future of personal fulfillment which is defined by the standards that you are setting for your life. Just making wishes, as you've learned in the previous chapter, is not enough. Knowing what you want and expecting to get it is different from wishful thinking. Your habits are just as important to manifesting your dream life as intention and planning are.

As much as it's important to understand how the law of attraction works in your favor, you also need to understand yourself better. After all, it is the journey of self-actualization that you're chasing—working toward the full realization of your true potential. There is another Universal law that you need to take into account. It is called the *law of cause and effect.*

That means that your thoughts, beliefs, and habits lead to an effect. In other words, they also create outcomes. Even your unconscious thoughts and beliefs lead to outcomes or effects in your life, which you will learn more about in the next chapter. So, if there are *effects* in your life that you are unhappy with, you can change them by changing the cause. It is, therefore, important for you to create habits that will support your manifesting goals.

In the next section, we will look at five excellent dark feminine habits to keep you on track with manifesting the life of your dreams and your inner empowered femme fatale. Keep this in mind as you progress: The path of manifesting what you desire is, therefore, also the path of personal transformation. We have to become a new version of ourselves to change the cause of our destiny.

By choosing to manifest our dark feminine energy we are also, therefore, choosing true empowerment, and are defining what success means to us individually. Real success should never be associated with how the world defines success for you—it is how you define success for yourself that truly matters (Sicinski, 2009).

Creating a Daily Ritual for Manifesting Dark Feminine Energy

How you start your day really counts. Knowing where you're going in life is a crucial femme fatale trait. Confidence is grounded in a strong sense of knowing exactly what you're going after and creating a habitual routine to support it. When you are uncertain, doubtful, frustrated, negative, and unclear, it will show up in many ways in your life. You will feel stuck and experience resentment, dissatisfaction, and unhappiness.

This is why creating daily rituals to support your ongoing manifesting will keep you inspired, energized, and positive. Every queen needs a magical ritual to uplift her, and so do you. It is important that you customize your rituals according to what inspires and enriches your life. Here are some ideas to get your day off to a great start.

Cultivate a Morning Ritual to Get in Touch With Your Divine Dark Feminine Energy

Exercise can also put us in touch with our intuition as much as meditation. Swimming, walking meditation, or earthing (spending time in nature) is a wonderful way of grounding yourself every morning. This is what strengthens our connection to our intuition. A femme fatale is reluctant to put her trust completely in others because she knows better—her best interests lie in getting in touch with her own higher self. We all have natural intelligence that we can connect to when we take time out to achieve that.

Starting your day connecting to higher intelligence is the same as connecting to your dark feminine energy. Trust in yourself above all others and follow the gentle nudges of intuition that you receive from your inner femme fatale daily. Intuition will not be logical at times, nor will it be based on socialized ideas. The spirit that lies within is an embodiment of dark and light feminine beyond your physical reality. Trust in it and let it flow freely and unburdened by negativity daily.

Energize Your Body, Mind, and Spirit With Your Own Dark Feminine Positivity Spell

Spells are meant to turn things around in your life. Creating your own daily positivity spell can be anything you set your mind on doing to keep you centered on positivity. Think of it as a way of bringing to life your dark feminine powers to eliminate traces of negativity. A positivity spell can be choosing one inspiring activity to accomplish daily.

For example, it can be setting aside at least 20 min in your day to listen to a guided meditation that helps uplift your mood. Another positivity spell could be using essential oils to enliven your environment, like a zesty orange or seductive ylang-ylang. Using essential oils is a wonderful way of using the power of scent to get in touch with your own seductive nature or to deepen your intuitive abilities.

All essential oils are made from plants and flowers, and their unique scents can help you feel anything from calming to empowering to seductive. They also stimulate the imagination and can induce visions of creativity. A dark feminine trait is originality. Femmes fatales are trendsetters and they revel in their unique creative potential. Creativity is the spark of originality.

Get in Touch With Your Authentic Self by Allowing Nature to Guide You

Nature is a wonderful reminder to us of our authenticity. Not only is it wonderfully soothing to notice nature, but it is also extremely grounding. Human nature is such that we often get lost in the delusions of the way things should be instead of observing how they really are. Nature brings us back down to Earth, to remind us of the thing that matters to us, not what matters to others. If you find peace in nature, you will find peace within.

Even just sitting outside for a few moments to observe the sunrise or the sunset will soothe our injured souls, and remind us of our authenticity. May the sky remind you of your unlimited potential, and of the freedom you can enjoy when you give yourself permission to be authentic—which is a natural combination of the spark of light and the taunt of the dark feminine energy.

Manifesting Your Beautiful Seductive Self

Whether you're single or in a relationship, seduction is the art of including playfulness in your relationship. It's also about you as a femme fatale getting in touch with your sensuality—an important ingredient for feeling desirable. Seduction is often associated with sex, but there is more to seduction than being sexual. It brings about a greater degree of confidence, and it also shapes how you feel about your sexuality. For example, if there are limited beliefs holding you back from being and feeling seductive, it will interfere with how you feel about your sexual identity as a woman.

Femmes fatales are very comfortable in their sexuality, and this is why Hollywood tends to exaggerate the power of seduction they have over men. Aim to feel comfortable in your sexuality first, and then start visualizing what kind of seduction you would love to express with your partner. When you are comfortable in your body and sensuality, being seductive will become second nature. Sometimes, we do get stuck in priorities and mundanity, and this is often what causes most people to neglect seeing value in seduction.

You can rekindle your seductive powers and nurture what is a striking quality of femmes fatales—their ability to seduce their partner and others around them with their charm, sense of individual style, sense of humor, playfulness, and remarkable confidence. Here's some great advice to manifest your beautiful, seductive self:

1. **Getting clear on your vision:** We must always start with achieving clarity on our vision of what being seductive means to us personally. Ask yourself: What are your ideas of being seductive? Once again, Hollywood does give us some important clues about how women can be seductive. So, we can take some of our cues from our favorite Hollywood femme fatales whom we admire.

   However, do go ahead and make a list of those women who you think adequately define what being seductive means to you. You can add other women to your list who are not Hollywood femmes fatales. Visualize how their seductive traits can be adapted to your lifestyle. These traits that you admire should strongly resonate with you.

2. **Act as if you are already seductive:** Imagine what it would be like to be as seductive as those women you admire. Your next step is to experiment with those ideas by implementing them. Have some fun with them and at the first opportunity start manifesting your seductive traits (the ones that resonate with you). Subtlety in seduction is very appealing as opposed to being over the top.

Play it out naturally and work your way to becoming more and more confident in your ability to feel confident about your sensuality. Always visualize how you want to be seductive with your crush or your partner. Imagine how you could flirt with them playfully and use your body language to let them know that you're confidently attracted to them. Visualizing your seductive goals will give you more confidence to start being more seductive.

3. **Develop traits to manifest your seductive self:** Pay attention to your current nature and start adopting more seductive qualities by implementing them as traits. Get in touch daily with your seductive side by challenging any belief or negative thoughts that you may be projecting that do not support being and feeling freer from within.

Our limiting thoughts and beliefs about who we are hold us back in many ways. Visualize that those limited beliefs no longer exist and you are comfortable with your sensuality and seductive powers. Seductiveness is enhanced when you are genuinely confident and secure within yourself. So, whatever is in the way, imagine that it isn't anymore.

How to Attract High-Value People Into Your Life

What do you think about the quality of people you currently engage with, and how would you define the qualities of high-value people? If you've experienced toxic relationships with others, or are currently battling things out in a toxic relationship, then you should instinctively know what does not constitute a high-value relationship. Without a doubt, having high-value people in your life can result in more equitable and satisfying relationships.

That is why we must aim to attract high-value people. The signs would be clear enough. They will support you in your goals and encourage you along the way. When you receive the right kind of support, it also gets easier to manifest your goals as high-value people help you to release the right frequency to attract what you want. Toxic and non-supportive people on the other hand will bring you down. That is inevitable because they do not have your best interests in mind.

1. **Getting clear on your vision:** Visualize having people in your life who respect and value you, and who see you as someone they regard highly. Everyone wants to be respected and valued for who they are, so it's not hard to imagine being with people who manifest these qualities. It is a most natural need inherent in all of us: to be with people who take us seriously and support us.

    Just be very clear that you want to attract more high-value people in your life and you will start seeing the red flags immediately when you are confronted by toxic people. It is important for you to visualize the traits that you regard as high value as this will eliminate people from your list right now who do not manifest what you regard as high value.

2.   **Act as if you are that already:** To attract high-value
     people in your life, you must also aim to be a high-value
     person. This means that you will not allow yourself to be
     disrespected, abused, used, or taken advantage of because
     high-value people do not regard those things as being
     acceptable by their high standards. Visualize that you will
     no longer tolerate being with anyone who disregards you,
     dismisses you, or puts you down.

     Envision yourself becoming the high-value person that you
     want to consistently attract in your life. If you are constantly
     putting up with people who you know are manipulative,
     uncaring, and disregarding your feelings, then you need to
     change that by spending as little time as possible with them
     or cutting them completely out of your life.

3.   **Traits and behavior to manifest high value in**
     yourself: Respect yourself, value yourself and your
     needs, and prioritize your life according to the things that
     you love doing. First learn to value everything about your
     life, your time, and your needs. When you value yourself,
     you will also value others more easily and give them the
     space to be themselves. You will feel more confident and
     deserving of happiness and success, and when you achieve
     this, you will also love to be surrounded by others who
     reflect high-value qualities.

     A high-value person is someone who has high standards
     and high expectations for happiness, success, love, and
     friendships. Loyalty, openness, sincerity, respect for self and

others, and healthy boundaries are all important ingredients to ensure high value and, therefore, high-quality relationships with others.

Manifesting Your Ideal Love Life

Here you would need to think about your ideal partner or soulmate. Have you given much thought to the traits you would love your ideal partner to possess? Just as you can manifest the life you deserve by focusing on your goals and mapping out a plan, you can attract your ideal partner. An important femme fatale trait is not settling for a partner who does not meet your expectations.

This is why you must also get clear on what your ideal partner will look like—in terms of their traits, the qualities you are seeking, and the life you may be seeking with them. Once you're clear, it will be easier for you to attract your ideal partner because you will automatically delist potential partners who do not live up to your high expectations.

1. **Getting clear on your vision:** Begin by describing the kind of person you would love to have as a partner. Give as much detail as possible in your list and be clear on why you think this person would be great for you. Just as you can manifest the life you deserve by focusing on your goals and mapping out a plan, you can attract your ideal partner.

    However, you must also get clear on what that ideal partner will look like—in terms of their traits, the qualities you are seeking, and the life you may be seeking with them. Once you're clear, it will be easier for you to find that ideal partner. Give as much detail as possible in your list and be clear on why you think this person would be great for you.

2. **Act as if you are already in that relationship with your ideal partner:** Script what your life is like right now with your ideal partner. Once you've experienced what it would feel like if you attracted your ideal partner in your life, vividly describe in your journal how this relationship is progressing as if it is already in existence. This is a very powerful way of manifesting what you want. You can also do visualization meditations daily when you think about your love life. Conjure up moments that you are already experiencing with your loved one.

   For example, picture watching a movie together all snuggled up together, and give details about the things you talk about and laugh about. What would be romantic moments for you and your partner to enjoy? Visualize different moments together daily that you are sharing with your partner as if you are already in that relationship.

3. **Inspiring visualization techniques to help you attract your ideal partner:** Visualization will help you manifest your daily partner. Have some fun and visualize future moments with your ideal partner. Femmes fatales are stricter with their requirements for their ideal partner than average women are, so pull out the stops when it

comes to setting high standards for yourself to attract your ideal partner.

Don't be afraid of flying solo until you've found your match! If you desire to have a relationship with a partner who is adventurous and who loves to travel a lot, then visualize how you will arrange your life to accommodate your traveling adventures with your ideal partner. Where would you travel to? Make a list of all the places you would love to explore in the world with your future catch, and add color and detail to your visualizations.

Overcoming Barriers to Manifesting

The process of manifestation is what you do to make your dreams come true. You have now learned how important it is not to block out your dark feminine energy, as it is key to achieving personal empowerment. Your femininity depends on achieving a healthy balance between your light and dark sides. Your shadow sides of your personality (the qualities that you repress) are key to manifesting your true desires.

It is the side of you that rebels against the things you do not want to experience, situations, and people who pull you down. This is why dark feminine energy is important to manifest in all areas of your life. It will show you what is truly important to you to live your best and most fulfilling life. When you experience resistance to achieving your manifesting goals, then that resistance is key to overcoming barriers to manifesting.

Resistance to manifesting anything that you want is inner friction caused by feelings of inadequacy. When you do not feel deserving of love, success, or unhappiness because you perceive yourself as being incapable or undeserving of achieving those things, then you will experience resistance. Those are the barriers to manifesting your goals and dreams. To overcome these barriers, you must fight for yourself and your right to enjoy happiness, love, and success.

The femme fatale in you must step up her game to shine, regardless of the inner friction and, hence, resistance that will come up to remind you that you still have some work to do on yourself. It was Carl Jung who famously quipped, "What you resist not only persists but will grow in size" (Goodreads, n.d.). Unless you face your fears and feelings of inadequacy, you will never conquer them fully.

This is the secret to overcoming barriers to manifesting your best life—being able to conquer your fears or transcend your circumstances. Coco Chanel, who revolutionized fashion for women, never had it easy. She had to overcome great trials and survive an intensely difficult childhood in the late 19th century. Chanel, like so many other women who persevered even when all the odds were stacked against them, depended on her strength and willpower to achieve great success.

She was sent to an orphanage penniless and a ward of the state when her father abandoned her. Her upbringing was not joyous.

She was lonely growing up alone in an orphanage, and she was poor. Chanel had no one to depend on besides the nuns at the orphanage who were hardly good at being a suitable confidante for a young girl.

The orphanage was rough. Still, she persevered and followed her dreams when she had more reason to feel insecure and down on luck. It was hard work and perseverance, and not resisting success that led to her legendary success. If you too would love to unleash that dark feminine determined energy, then you can start right now by taking a few moments to answer the following questions. It will help you to achieve more clarity on the life you want to manifest. There's a femme fatale trailblazer within you that is waiting to emerge.

1. What would happen if you don't give yourself a chance to make the changes you need to?

2. What would happen if you did give yourself a chance to make positive, more inspiring changes in your life?

3. What would happen if you did not conquer your fears to do what you want, regardless of the feelings of inadequacy you experience?

4. What would happen if you do not give yourself permission to find your ideal partner?

5. What would happen if you do not commit to succeeding and improving in your field of profession?

6. What would happen if you do not take certain chances on yourself and just do more of the things that you love to do?

7. What would happen if you consistently believe the negative self-talk that makes you feel undeserving and undervalued?

8. What would happen if you continuously allowed yourself to be devalued by others?

9. What would happen if you remain accepting toxic relationships because you don't feel worthy of enjoying high-value and high-quality relationships?

10. What would happen if you always shine your light feminine energy in the world without allowing your stronger traits to manifest? (Think back on moments when you didn't say no, when you did not honor your true feelings, and when you failed to assert yourself.)

As you aim to answer these questions that are designed to help you to stop resisting the things that you want to achieve, keep in mind that awareness is key to change. Make it a point of close paying attention to your thoughts, feelings, and emotions. Constantly examine why resistance comes up for you. For example, if you fail to answer a job ad because it makes you nervous to market yourself and your skills, then you are most likely feeling inadequate about your ability to achieve success.

It also means that you have some work to do on yourself to increase your self-confidence and self-esteem. Give yourself permission to battle it out subconsciously with the negative feelings that come up that are working against you because if you don't overcome those barriers, you will remain stuck and your manifesting progress will be hindered by those negative thoughts and beliefs about yourself and your abilities. Here are some ways to overcome barriers to manifesting the life you deserve:

- **Switch the internal dialogue from negative to positive**: When a negative thought comes up that negates your abilities or devalues you, then turn it wound to a positive thought. Push down those negatives and allow your inner femme fatale to take over to push you in the direction that you need to take to advance in your manifesting goals.

- **Avoid procrastination:** Make your goals your priority and stick with them. When you find yourself being slowed down in any way whatsoever, readjust your lifestyle to ensure that you are making adequate time to focus on manifesting your goals.

- **Meditate daily:** Do not skip this part, because it is during meditation that we will hear the voices of both our light and dark feminine sides. Depending on the situation, one will win over the other. Trust your intuition and keep in mind that if something doesn't feel empowering, don't do it. Meditation will keep your energies balanced and it will allow you to get in touch with a much higher wisdom from within.

- Meditation, just like exercise, leads to the production of serotonin and endorphins (otherwise known as happy hormones). These hormones stimulate more feelings of security, positivity, and creativity. These feelings are most likely to push you more in the direction of those things that are important to you (Whitener, 2022).

Patience and Trusting the Universe

Patience is a virtue, and trusting in your ability to succeed is the elixir to manifesting what you want. While it is not a long shot to expect quick results in some of the manifests you will be doing, the rule is that things happen in their own time. So, place your trust in yourself and the Universe that all good things come to those who are patient. Believing in yourself must top the agenda of your manifesting goals. There will be challenges along the way and setbacks, and some of those challenges and setbacks may be totally out of your control.

This is why being realistic about your expectations is important. It includes taking into account factors that may have nothing to do with you but with others or situations that you did not foresee. Always go into anything keeping in mind that there will be pros and cons that you will encounter in every new situation aligned with your manifesting goals. Be willing to make adjustments and enjoy the journey of self-discovery that will unfold as you progress in your journey.

CLOSING AFFIRMATION:

I am a powerful, capable, and empowered woman on a mission to realize my fullest and greatest potential.

SECRET #3

Becoming an Empowered
Femme Fatale

*The more I see the sea, the more I want to give myself
away to its lovely current. But then I realized. I am
the current. I am the sea. It is that what is me.*

– Wald Wassermann

Inner Transformation and Manifestation

Everything that you want to achieve, manifest, and experience begins with the journey of nurturing complete confidence in yourself. In other words, if you lack self-confidence, you will undoubtedly fail to realize your greatest potential. A lack of self-confidence holds us back in life.

When you begin to do the inner work of transformation, you will notice upon closer reflection how you may have let opportunities slip by because of a lack of self-confidence. It does not have to be your continuous reality. You can change that. It takes confidence to have tenacity and to keep moving in the direction of your dreams even when you're at your lowest.

It takes confidence to say, "I will try again tomorrow," when things look bleak—life is not a bed of roses. The defining factor that will guarantee your success is having confidence in yourself and your ability not just to succeed, but to overcome setbacks. This is the accomplishment of women who have done the work of inner transformation. They keep pushing through their setbacks—that is confidence!

A femme fatale builds her success on having supreme self-confidence and her ability to transcend all limiting thoughts, beliefs, and circumstances. This is the work of inner transformation. It takes a lot of guts at times to challenge the status quo and, sometimes, it comes at a high cost.

Femme fatale women are not as hard as nails. Just like everyone else, they too feel the complexity of their emotions when challenges arise. We've all experienced the pain of limiting self-beliefs and the trauma of being rejected, but we also grew from those experiences, and you know already that if you allow limiting self-beliefs to persist, your self-confidence will be constantly bashing.

Femmes fatales were also in that same boat at some point in their life, but they decided to change their mindset—to hold a strong and compelling vision for themselves in their mind's eye. That vision will always be the overriding factor when things get tough. They also chose to believe in themselves above everything else and to keep going after what is important to them.

Femmes fatales are not born. The hard knocks of life have led them down that path of inner transformation, and this is how they began to connect with their dark feminine energy. Our dark feminine energy calls out to us when we need to create change in our life when we are angry, and when we know we deserve so much better.

Femmes fatales have used their pain to channel their dark feminine energy appropriately to powerfully manifest their desires: Femmes fatales are feisty and determined women who see value in themselves even when they hit low points in their life. The fictional character of femme fatales being invincible is unrealistic. Femmes fatales are not invincible, but they are women of remarkable strength of character. This is how they are more than capable of overcoming both inner and outer limitations.

It is the dark feminine energy magic that keeps them on this path of inner transformation and personal empowerment. It is the energy of passion, creativity, and fiery contemplation—it is not passive and blissful like the energy of your light side of compassion and love.

Femmes fatales are deeply connected to this side of their feminine power and they put in the hours of hard work holding themselves accountable for the results they wish to manifest.

If you trace the lifestyle choices, habits, and writings of some of the most accomplished women who have lived on the planet, you will discover these traits: hardworking, deeply passionate, and committed to their causes. They do not compare themselves to others and they simply set out to do what they love, regardless of what may come their way to disrupt their plans. They are confident, smart, and crafty, and they do not waste their time on people or projects that are not aligned with what is most important to them.

All of the great women who made a whopping success for themselves possessed femme fatale traits. This means that those who go for what they are after are perfectly confident, rebellious, tenacious, and determined to succeed. However, it is true, these women also paid a price to reach this stage of development. They made sacrifices to get to the top of their field of expertise. Success comes at a price too. They also had to face their fears to overcome the limitations of their reality.

They gave themselves hope, yet felt every shed of the pain associated with taking a stand for what they believed in. Open any biography book on successful women and you will start seeing a pattern: clarity of vision, plan of action, shifting of beliefs, determination, sacrifice, hard work, confidence, and success!

Manifesting your dark feminine energy is, therefore, a lifelong journey that requires constant evaluation, and reevaluation of your thoughts, beliefs, attitudes, and choices. This chapter is all about doing that inner work to become an empowered femme fatale. Faking it is not going to cut it for you. So, do keep this in mind in your journey of inner transformation: You can journal and state affirmations all day long, but if your actions and character don't reflect what you want to manifest, it won't work.

Ultimately, it will be your attitude, choices, and character that will determine your ability to channel the dark feminine energy to create the results you are seeking (in every choice and decision that you make for yourself).

Confidence Is Your Default but It's Easy to Forget

We've all had moments of confidence and moments of weakness—so, we get it already that life is an ebb and flow of different challenges and opportunities. The amount of confidence you can feel at any point in time also depends on so many factors but when you closely examine your state of mind and level of confidence, it is not hard to get to the root cause of the issues that may be bringing your self-confidence down.

Things that may have occurred to us in the past that were traumatic and still unresolved to this day will continue to let us down. Trauma can make it hard to be confident all the time, so it makes it easy to forget that confidence is your default.

Even when we know that we are so worthy of feeling strong and confident, we can let ourselves down by allowing negativity and old emotional patterns to get in the way. It is possible to heal those past issues and to decide that you can have the final say in all matters of your life, including the outcome of every challenging situation.

Confidence is also your ability to keep going even when you are not feeling excited, enthused, and bubbling with anticipation. If you choose to be a driving force behind your victory, you will not place so much emphasis on failure. When you are lacking in confidence, it is the fear of failure at an unconscious level that may be holding you back.

Once again, even femmes fatales feel anxious, nervous at times about their future, and self-conscious. They are not invincible beings of dark feminine power. However, they are super-conscious of the importance of having the final say in their destiny. They choose empowerment over the fear of failure—that will always be the winning factor in the game of confidence. It is the fear of failure that is often at the core of low self-confidence and self-esteem.

A femme fatale deep down knows she's valuable and capable, so even if there are moments of personal weaknesses that come up, they are able to override the negativity in their life. A femme fatale understands that confidence is her default state—her true self. So, she understands her negative feelings, how to process them, work through them with self-compassion, and move past them.

The Relationship Between Self-Confidence and Self-Esteem

Self-esteem is how we feel about ourselves, and self-confidence is the reaction to self-esteem. So, if we feel great about our identity, traits, quirks, beliefs, outlook, attitude, and choices, our self-esteem will be at a healthy level. On the other hand, low feelings of self-esteem are associated with low levels of self-confidence. Fear of failure is the link between both low self-esteem and self-confidence. It is important to heal feelings of low self-confidence and low self-esteem.

If your confidence is taking a hit because of your ongoing fear of failure, it will hinder your progress at manifesting your dark feminine traits to help you succeed at a faster and more determined rate. Your motivation will fall because of the negative self-talk that recurs in your mind, resulting from fear of failure. Sometimes, that fear of failure may be linked to trauma or society's pressure on women. Overcoming past trauma and societal expectations will be your number one challenge to regaining self-confidence and self-esteem.

Mainly, these two issues are what causes many foxy women to lose their natural state of confidence. However, if you commit to healing from those issues, you will be able to bounce back. If you've experienced severe trauma in the past and are struggling to overcome them, seeking the help of a mental health care professional will help. Awareness is the first step to recognizing that there are mental health issues that you need to address.

Mental health issues will always pull us down in life unless we can turn the light on them and do the work to address all underlying issues. Trauma can be related to mental, physical, or emotional abuse of any kind. Trauma left untreated can lead to feelings of shame, guilt, and even self-hate (Cherry, 2023).

For example, if you grew up in an unsupportive family with parents who called you names and belittled you, then the abuse would've undoubtedly been traumatic to a young person still forming their identity. Other kinds of abuse can also result in self-doubt and self-hate, especially if you were not in touch with your dark feminine energy and kept taking it and taking it, without challenging the abuse.

All that emotional pain and pent-up feelings damages our brain and can result in long-term self-esteem and self-confidence issues. However, due to the neuroplastic nature of the brain (the ability to heal and adapt), the damage can be reversed.

This is why it is important to shine a light on the causes of low self-confidence. We all know what they are. It is about having the courage to face them and heal them. The same approach must be followed when dealing with societal expectations of women, which can also lead to trauma. When women are not in touch with their dark feminine energy, it becomes challenging to take a stand for what they believe in.

Most women who are not in touch with their dark feminine side will struggle to assert themselves. This too creates trauma, stress, and mental health issues, especially when values, societal constructs, and outdated beliefs about a woman's place in the world are thrust upon them in a dictatorial manner.

Regaining Your Self-Confidence

It is not rocket science to go about regaining your self-confidence. The greater your connection is with your dark feminine power, the easier it becomes to pick yourself up from any painful, or challenging situation. Self-belief is key to regaining self-confidence. You can start here with this one simple step: Be kind to yourself.

Femmes fatales get this easily (what it means to be kind to themselves) and this is why they can bounce back quickly when facing setbacks: They do not internalize issues and they treat themselves with kindness, compassion, and reverence (not in a narcissistic way—as that is associated with low self-esteem). Femmes fatales love to pick themselves up again without the need to become clingy and dependent on others to give them support. They revel in their ability to bounce back from setbacks.

They are quick to find their inner strength and apply it to areas in their life that need transformation. Femmes fatales know that self-confidence is also about showing kindness and empathy to themselves when issues come up to challenge them. Aligning yourself and your actions to a personal code of integrity, authenticity, and self-belief will help you to regain confidence in those areas of your life where you feel a sense of lack.

Think of the things that you will say to a friend who is going through a low self-confidence phase, and apply that wisdom to yourself. You can make a list of all those things that are bringing you down, and next to each one of them, write a positive aspect of yourself that you like, admire, respect, and celebrate!

Self-Esteem

Self-esteem has everything to do with how we view ourselves, think about ourselves, and regard our personal brand representation to the world. Remember that everything that you think, feel, and decide to act upon is a reflection of how you feel about yourself.

One of the first things a femme fatale recognizes is her innate ability to accept herself, honor her personal and physical identity, and enjoy the uniqueness that she brings to all situations in her thinking and behavior patterns. Nathaniel Branden's book, *The Six Pillars of Self-Esteem*, has become a leading authority on this subject for good reason. It focuses on the important aspects that address self-esteem, which are:

1. **Living consciously:** This requires being aware of how you regard yourself, deal with people, how you prioritize your daily activities, and your approach to resolving daily conflict within

yourself. For example, if you are not happy with your physical appearance, you must start healing those negative thoughts about yourself and practice more self-acceptance.

2. **Self-acceptance:** Without self-acceptance, your days will be filled with anxiety, stress, and negative images of who you are. Femmes fatales are their own best friend, and you must aim to cultivate this relationship with yourself. Encourage yourself, inspire yourself, and tell yourself how wonderful you are regularly because that is what friends do.

They support, love, and inspire positive growth opportunities for those they love and value. Do this for yourself, and keep moving forward toward accepting those qualities of yourself that you may despise. We develop negative ways of thinking about ourselves when we reinforce them with negative thoughts, feelings, and actions.

3. **Self-responsibility:** Accountability is what makes us responsible for our thoughts, beliefs, choices, and actions. If you notice that they are not properly aligned to supporting a positive identity about yourself, then adjust them accordingly. When you make a mistake or have a moment that is not reflective of the inner wisdom of your dark feminine self, be kind and supportive instead of self-negating. It is a question of taking responsibility immediately and aligning with your dark feminine side, which is more action-orientated than indulging in self-pity or self-hate.

4. **Self-assertiveness:** You can only achieve greatness when you recognize the need to assert yourself at times. This should be a natural reaction when confronting people who are not supportive or aligned with your values, integrity, and expectations. Yes, it is important to have healthy and high expectations of yourself and others and to communicate those expectations assertively when boundaries are crossed, and when you're disrespected.

5. **Living purposefully:** Living according to your highest values and inner callings will ultimately determine the importance that you give to them. Self-acceptance includes being accountable to yourself to ensure that you are not neglecting to be purposeful because this is what will bring you feelings of fulfillment. It will also raise the bar on how you feel about yourself and your ability to achieve greatness in your areas of expertise.

6. **Practicing integrity:** When your values, beliefs, and actions are all aligned, you will achieve personal integrity. If you love, respect, and value yourself, you will also stop putting yourself down. When you recognize the importance of respecting your code of integrity, you will feel liberated from within and you will develop a stronger self-identity. Knowing what you believe in and what it means to you practically is an important way of feeling good about who you are as a woman totally in charge of her life (Branden, 1994).

Self-Love

Self-love is your ability to love and respect yourself by putting yourself first. Honoring your needs and reflecting on your level of self-confidence and self-esteem is also an act of self-love. Taking time out daily to engage in self-care activities that improve feelings of love, joy, and personal fulfillment is also an act of self-love. Healing your past trauma is an act of self-love—so is prioritizing your life according to your hierarchy of values.

This is not hard to follow at all, especially when you're manifesting more of your dark feminine energy. There are lots of women today who identify with the need to make themselves a priority. They achieve this by honoring their dark feminine energy and saying no to things that are not important to them.

Even if you're going through a rough patch right now, just holding the light of love and hope in your vision will do the trick of shifting your mindset to one of self-love. Adding even a modicum of hope to your outlook every day will brighten things up for you and increase your vibrational frequency. As you've already learned—feeling amazing about who you are will uplift your vibrational frequency—this will speed up the manifesting process. Think of self-love as a dark feminine energy spell that you can put on yourself every day to achieve more happiness, greater fulfillment, and joy in life.

Make a list of the things that you love doing that will increase feelings of self-confidence and self-appreciation, then go out and do those things. That is your self-love femme fatale spell! Keep yourself feeling good about who you are and what you aim to accomplish, and keep moving in that direction.

This is how you best express your authentic self—by making those choices every day that support your goals and uplifts your self-esteem. Keep yourself in your spotlight, and love being there because that is what harnesses more of that magical dark feminine energy that will see you growing, thriving, and succeeding.

Setting Boundaries

When you set meaningful boundaries for yourself, you are harnessing the qualities of your inner femme fatale. It should become a priority to say no more often than not. Sometimes, we adopt people-pleasing behavior because it makes us feel good about ourselves helping others. However, you will soon learn how time-consuming it can be to constantly be a *good woman*.

You will start feeling drained, resentful, and people will take advantage—because that is just the nature of people. Once you put yourself out there as a people pleaser—someone who is always available to listen to others' problems, help them out, and even do time-consuming favors—you will be setting a trap for yourself and minimizing yourself.

A people pleaser is saying to the world, "I don't value my time, resources, and self as much as I value you and yours." Always be mindful of how you spend your time and how much of it you are willing to give to others. Unless they are living with you and make up a vital part of your personal life, reconsider your motivation when overextending yourself to help others out. Even taking on extra work can be a people-pleasing reaction to requests. We all get only 24 hr in a day, so how you spend your time is a crucial factor to take into account when looking at your goals.

The same logic should apply to who you spend time with—are you in friendships or relationships with people (work and personal) who are toxic? Ask yourself: Do you consider any of your relationships as bad relationships? If you have identified bad relationships, then your next step would be to set up some boundaries with those people.

For example, you can decide to limit the amount of time that you spend with them, or if it is a very bad situation, you can decide to completely cut those people out of your life. It is not always possible or relevant to cut people out of your life. You must assess each situation and connect with your inner femme fatale when making that choice.

Acting confidently, decisively, and wisely is what you must aim for—trust your gut instinct! It is the dark feminine power that will guide you to set healthy boundaries with people. Healthy boundaries are important to maintain, even in relationships that are going well for you. Making time for yourself and also balancing how you spend your time with others are important considerations.

When you compromise on your self-care time, for example, it is also regarded as a people-pleasing choice. Prioritize the amount of time you spend with others as a secondary activity that follows on the back of fulfilling your priorities. Make it a femme fatale rule: I will not let anyone drag me down, manipulate me, or take advantage of me or my valuable time.

Shadow Work

It was Carl Jung who introduced the world to shadow work. He referred to the shadows of our personality as small parts that we disowned as a result of a personal judgment that we passed on ourselves. Due to forming limiting judgments about these shadow traits, we pushed them aside to hide them from our awareness. These small shadow parts represent our sorrow, our perceived lack, and our insecurities.

Let's use a hypothetical example: Let's say that when you were young, you may have been overweight. This could've resulted in you disliking yourself because you were overweight, so you ejected your overweight version of who you were in the shadows. Meanwhile, you kept an obsessive eating plan to ensure that you never had to be the overweight girl you once were in the past.

This is the story of many young women today struggling with weight issues to fit in and be more attractive and "acceptable." They look at images of slimmer girls who are popular and fashionable and they start detesting themselves because of their perceived inadequacy for being overweight. The consequence of body-shaming themselves is personal rejection and refusal to love and accept themselves as they are.

When you reject a part of who you are, it remains in your subconscious mind and becomes a part of your psyche. This rejection continues to cause psychological discomfort. Even if you are doing better physically, the chances are quite strong that your feelings of insecurity related to your weight issue will linger in your subconscious mind.

You will also develop eating disorders or a very unhealthy relationship with food as a result of this shadow rejection of yourself. These repressed parts of our personality, therefore, represent the darker side of who we once were. We feel ashamed of these parts and never quite "own them." When we reject even small parts of who we are, that energy frequency stays with us and makes us feel more rejected and insecure. Another consequence would be living with ongoing weight issues for many years thereafter.

Unless we heal those rejected aspects of ourselves and start owning the shadow parts of our personality, we will remain stuck at an unconscious level and we will not progress. It is more liberating to own your shadow self and to accept the overweight version of yourself with unconditional love. Shadow work, therefore, involves calling out to your dark inner shadows—those parts of your personality that you previously rejected.

The work includes honoring and making peace with the rejected parts of who you once were. It includes loving those parts of who you were and integrating them into yourself to feel more whole, loved, and healed. Essentially, the healing involves no longer hating yourself or those parts of yourself. The shadow work, therefore, corrects your previous rejection of parts of yourself that were unacceptable to you.

There are a lot of expectations that people themselves have placed on females throughout the generations. Whenever you aim to meet the expectations of others, you will push certain parts of your personality away into the shadows—those parts that do not conform to the standards set by others. When you do this, you begin rejecting parts of yourself. You can heal those parts of yourself by getting in touch with your shadows (Wright, 2022).

Shadow Work Journaling Prompts

Journaling is a great way to begin doing the shadow work on yourself. I have developed a list of prompts to get you started. Set aside some time every day to work through these prompts. Give yourself adequate time to allow for revelations to come to the surface, and be patient with the insights that will be revealed as you progress through the work. You can do this on your personal computer, or you can use a notepad (whichever feels more comfortable for you).

During the process, make sure that you will not have any interruptions. Allow your thoughts to flow and connect to your feelings. Articulate your feelings properly onto the paper on which you are writing or the page on which you are typing. Keep in mind that when you are being reflective, you might experience heavy feelings from the past associated with your rejected parts. If it becomes too intense for you, you can walk away from the exercise and come back to it.

Also, throughout the process, keep in mind the importance of connecting to the dark feminine energy within. It seeks to be acknowledged. Your dark feminine energy will manifest as healing wisdom and insight that is not grounded in the societal constructs that once formed part of your identity. If you are only concerned with the light feminine energy, then this might have also resulted in suppressing parts of you.

Pay attention to how you feel about your past, the choices you made, and the manifestation of those choices. If you were overly concerned about making the right impression on others, then you were disregarding the wisdom of your dark feminine side. The light feminine side manifests in its way; however, there must always be a balance in your choices that reflects both the dark feminine energy and the light feminine energy, or you risk being mercilessly taken advantage of.

The key to shadow work is to practice compassion for yourself because the dark feminine is compassionate and on your side. The dark feminine energy is the protective layer of your intuition to challenge what does not feel right for you and you alone. Now that you better understand the process of doing shadow work and what you may most likely encounter, here are some journaling prompts to get you started on this life-transforming adventure! (Wright, 2022).

1. How did my parents bring me up?

2. How did I feel as a child growing up—understood or misunderstood?

3. How am I like my parents?

4. How am I not like my parents?

5. Have I repeated family patterns in my own life?

6. In what ways did I disagree with my parents?

7. What were the main causes of rebellious behavior?

8. How did I implement my values and beliefs into my adult life?

9. If I could advise my child-self, what would I say to her?

10. Will I tell my child-self the truth about the mistakes I made?

11. Did I respect my child-self by listening to what she wanted in life?

12. What parts of my life story will I not share with my child-self?

13. What parts of my life story will I emphasize to my child-self?

14. When in my life did I experience true peace with myself?

15. What do you think your child-self wishes for you now as a woman to experience?

16. What are the biggest obstacles in your path to finding true happiness now in your life?

17. What did your child-self fantasize about womanhood?

18. Have you lived up to your expectations?

19. Do you feel worthy of that dream, or has it evolved into something else now?

20. How do you define success today?

Becoming Independent

Whether you were brought up to be codependent or not, every woman should know from experience already the importance of gaining full independence for her thoughts, choices, and lifestyle. It makes you unique and helps you to stand out for your uniqueness. Being part of the crowd is as good as acknowledging a lack of personal growth and true empowerment. Being independent is the defining trait of a femme fatale who is truly in touch with her dark feminine energy.

A femme fatale does not feel uncomfortable in her presence alone. She is not lonely because there is so much going on in her life that there's never a dull moment to consider being lonely. Also, finding her ideal partner is not a priority but something that she has given much thought to, and, therefore, a femme fatale is never in a hurry to "settle down" through marriage.

A femme fatale gives her own definition of life and happiness and does not see the wisdom of marrying anyone to fulfill anyone else's expectations. She does not see marriage and landing the perfect partner that will impress others as her greatest victory. Her idea of life is to ensure her happiness, her independent pursuits, and to stand out and be noticed as a powerful woman in her own right! She wants to attract a partner who will continuously dazzle her and appreciate her as an individual (for who she is more than just being taken by her looks only).

She aims to be herself completely according to the manifestation of her definition of "sexy," and she also has a powerful say in the direction of her life and relationships. A femme fatale is always confident. She is not a woman who will be easily pushed back or pushed around. If a relationship is over, there is less of a chance of her going back to something in her past that ended, unless there are compelling reasons to do so.

Femmes fatales are not dictators, but they value themselves completely first and foremost, especially when in a romantic and sexual relationship with someone else. She knows when it's time to move on from a relationship that has become unsatisfying for her, one that no longer holds her interest. She is not a hypocrite nor does a femme fatale care about staying in a relationship for the "sake of making an ongoing impression on society," or anyone else for that matter.

Usually, women who are not in touch with their dark feminine energy will stay in unsatisfying relationships to maintain an ongoing status quo. Also, they are fearful for themselves and others to be independent and break away on their own from unsatisfying relationships.

A femme fatale, on the other hand, believes in taking inspired action every day (whether she is in a relationship or not) to manifest things that are important to her. She has a plan of action and a career, and she is creatively involved in things in her life that are of great value to her and the time and effort that she puts into things.

A femme fatale knows what she wants, she has goals and plans for her life, and she keeps moving in the direction of those goals and plans. She operates at her best when she is not in a comfort zone, because that always leaves the door open for growth, expansion, and new possibilities. Being independent is what makes her unstoppable.

Creating an Aura of Mystery Around Yourself

Another important trait of a femme fatale is how she communicates. As a confident, graceful, and powerful being of light and dark feminine energy, her communication style exudes this quality. In other words, she gives off a sense of complete independence while being warm and comfortable in her skin.

You will not get someone who lacks self-assurance, depth, charm, and knowledge on subjects that are important to her when communicating with a femme fatale. She has a few trusted individuals that she knows she can confide in. But she doesn't share her deepest thoughts and feelings with just anyone. She chooses who she confides in carefully.

A femme fatale does not wear her heart on her sleeve, as she sees it necessary to share everything that she is up to with everyone who crosses her path. Her friendships are therefore as purposeful as her life is and she keeps people who are reliable, dependable, and on her wavelength close to her. The last thing that femme fatale needs in their life is needy and clingy friends.

She is her boss. Her aloofness and ability to remain independent, secretive (when necessary), and non-committal create a remarkable aura of mystery around her. However, she is a good listener and she values intelligent and thoughtful conversations with others.

Her accomplishments are authentic and, therefore, make a natural impression on others. A femme fatale values her time and space and also values the wisdom that *less is more*—she will, therefore, withdraw timeously from large gatherings without overstaying her welcome or coming across as if she was dependent on anyone. Humility is her hallmark—her presence, warmth, amiability, wisdom, and intelligence graces her wherever she goes.

She wears these traits like a crown on her head, knowing that her presence must always be fitting of leaving a worthy impression on others (one that genuinely resonates with her femme fatale self). She regards her time, intellect, and wisdom as the presence of royalty, and behaves like a strong and remarkable queen in her own right.

CLOSING AFFIRMATION:
I am always deeply in touch with my dark feminine energy, that space where love and wisdom collide to bring me the happiness that I am worthy of receiving!

SECRET #4

Connecting to Dark Feminine Energy Through Sexuality and Pleasure

If you were born without wings do nothing to prevent them from growing.

– Coco Chanel

The Lost Art of Indulgence

D ark feminine energy is connected to a woman's body. A true femme fatale isn't afraid of indulging in pleasure, that's part of what makes spending time with her so exciting. Once you get in touch with your dark feminine energy, you will begin to understand why it is also closely related to a woman's sexuality and sensuality. Indulgence is often connected to our sensual nature. Indulgence is as pleasurable as sex.

The dark feminine energy is not only a seductive, sensual force of creativity and self-expression, but it is also a force that will lure you to pleasurable experiences, and that is an invitation that you should not resist. However, when caught in the throes of the indulgent nature of your dark feminine energy, do keep in mind that moderation is key to achieving happiness and balance.

Overindulgence can lead to the experience of the negative side of the dark feminine. Just as the light feminine side when overindulged will lead to negative consequences, so too can overindulge in the dark feminine energy. Be guarded about overstepping the balance between the two feminine forces and you will enjoy being indulgent without going over the top.

There's a difference between binging and indulging. One is mindless and compulsive, the other is an art. The last queen of France is a good example to use in the context of knowing the difference between the two. At first, her indulgence was an art and it impressed upon the king of France that his queen was able to entertain their royal guests and bring about social reform at Versailles.

However, as Queen Marie Antoinette persisted with her art, she became more extreme and knew no limits to her indulgence. She eventually became known throughout Europe during the 18th century for being so indulgent that France's eventual bankruptcy was blamed entirely on her and her husband's inability to reign her in. The working class was looking for scapegoats for their poverty in a feudal system prevalent throughout Europe, and the queen of France was the perfect reason to set the country on fire with revolt and violent opposition to their ill-fated destiny.

She's widely known for saying, "Let them eat cake," to the poor middle class who could no longer afford to eat bread and were starving. Her insensitivity maddened them even further and, as history shows, it fanned the flames of rage against the monarchy of France. Once adored but later beheaded, the last queen of France played the striking role of femme fatale without a limit to her indulgences, which led to her beheading. Once adored but later despised, the extreme level of indulgence she engaged in lost her favor amongst the masses and guaranteed her beheading.

Let there be limits to your indulgence, as you too will lose the respect you deserve for your bold and unique approach to manifesting your best life, which must be defined by reverence and not careless and reckless behavior. Eat cake but don't bust your diet or self-care routine. Dance the night away but don't consume too much alcohol as this could make you vulnerable and you might wake up the next morning regretting your behavior, especially if you ended up being more out of control than your usual self.

It is also unhealthy, unsexy, and irresponsible. Letting your guard down can easily destroy your reputation and diminish your position as a woman of stature, power, influence, class, and mystery.

How to Indulge Without Letting Yourself Go

Being mindful is key to enjoying life without becoming extreme in your quest to have fun. The radiance of the dark feminine energy can be accomplished when you are balanced from within. Mindfulness will allow you the pleasure of enjoying life to the fullest without attracting negative results. Know your limits and keep in mind that winning long-term should be more of a focus instead of indulging excessively in one single moment. Savor each moment of indulgence delightfully, but be mindful of not making it a long-term way of life.

The queen of France, for example, loved eating pastries and cakes, drinking champagne, and shopping for the latest designer fashionable attire. However, you may not have the same budget as the queen of France, and following a diet of high sugar content is not wise. Therefore, be mindful of priorities according to your own value system and don't break your commitment to it. You can still have fun in moderation. Make it your middle name. Here's how you can practice mindfulness when indulging, especially when dining out (Willard, 2019):

- **Slow down when consuming food or drink:** Be mindful of the taste and flavor, and indulge with your full senses.

- **Know your body's hunger signals:** Eat when you're hungry instead of eating to be social. Sometimes, emotions may guide us to be overindulgent. Be aware of what is driving your hunger or thirst.

- **Cultivate a mindful approach to where you eat:** Sometimes, we eat while on the go, or while cooking in the kitchen, we snack throughout the process. Avoid doing these things, as you are not being mindful of what you are eating, nor will you be able to enjoy your food intake.

- **Know the difference:** This is important when choosing between foods that are nutritious and those that are not when indulging. You will feel better indulging in healthier choices and can avoid feeling bloated.

- **Set your limits in advance:** If you're dining out, make sure that you are not starved and do not go over one glass of alcohol, especially if you're attending a formal event. Savor the company, and choose your food wisely.

The Role of Sexuality in Dark Feminine Energy

It's not just about the bedroom, it's about relishing life. We all have sexual energy to explore. This sexual energy is undoubtedly connected to the dark feminine energy within you. Sexuality, sensuality, and creativity are all interlinked to the dark feminine energy, and there is nothing more beautiful than a woman who reaches the peak of her awareness of this.

A woman's sexuality is the driving force of her power. Her sexuality should not be underrated as it often is by people who are more in touch with their light energy—this just applies to both men and women who are quick to negate a woman who is proud of her sexuality and openly expressive in the manner in which she walks, talks makes eye contact and dresses.

Femmes fatales are expressive because they are in touch with their sexual energy. It is the sexual energy that ignites the flame of passion, and we need passion to feel the ecstasy of being alive with potential. It comes naturally for femme fatales because they are confident and sexually liberated from within. Sexual energy is also associated with being spiritual. If you think of creation, the entire act of love and sexuality comes to mind.

This is the link that connects sexuality to the divine nature of our existence and the natural attraction we feel toward others who please us. Therefore, there is nothing to feel afraid of when it comes to sexuality. By nature, we are drawn to those whom we find attractive. It may not always be due to their physical body, but their energetic frequency, intelligence, or how they speak.

Sexual attraction is part of our nature. Leaving out the divine presence will lead to regarding sexual encounters as one that is lacking in feeling, and sacredness. Everyone that you engage with sexually involves their divine presence. The dark feminine is naturally (and powerfully, at times) evoked, using meaningful sexual encounters that establish a connection with body, mind, and spirit. We are attracted to sex and then we are attracted to each other because sex is a primal and sacred part of our existence and creation.

If you do find it uncomfortable coming to terms with your sexual energy, then it will require the question of what factors have caused that discomfort. Everyone is unique in their sexual expression. What may be considered moderate and acceptable for some may not be enough for someone else. It is up to you to define your sexual boundaries according to your personal sexual preferences. Be comfortable exploring what sexuality and sexual expression mean to you, keeping in mind your true feelings and thoughts on the subject.

CLOSING AFFIRMATION:

I am confident that the dark feminine energy within will guide me naturally to fully embrace my sexuality and sensuality in a manner that feels right for me!

SECRET #5

The Lifestyle of a Femme Fatale—It's Not Just Where You Are but Where You're Going

Ignore the glass ceiling and do your work. If you're focusing on the glass ceiling, focusing on what you don't have, focusing on the limitations, then you will be limited.

–Ava DuVernay

Where you are going counts, especially when it is important and meaningful to you. This is why a femme fatale pays attention to every little detail of her life. She does this because she understands the importance of following this simple formula for success: What you put in is what you will get out. Therefore, to support the ongoing manifestation of your goals, you need to also put energy into following a healthy lifestyle that will consistently bring you the results you desire.

Being healthy is key to achieving massive personal transformation. Health includes physical, emotional, psychological, and spiritual well-being. Aim for this and you will be amazed at how the entire quality and trajectory of your personal growth will be impacted.

If you want to look and feel great from the inside out, then you must begin the journey of transformation by doing an audit of your lifestyle. Your next step would be to create a list of all your current habits that are not serving you for your highest good and growth. For example, if looking and feeling great is an important goal, then eating junk food and not exercising regularly will not bring about the desired change that you want to manifest in your life.

Once you've identified the habits that you need to "kick" to become healthy, your next step is to implement meaningful changes to accommodate the manifestation of the desired outcome.

By tapping into your dark feminine energy, you can invite a new lifestyle vision into your life and start working with it daily to manifest your inner femme fatale image. Take delight in the vision you hold for yourself, indulge in it, embrace it fully, and pour love into it every day. Here are some amazing insights on the kind of lifestyle that femmes fatales follow based on their mindset, which is undoubtedly aligned with embracing the dark feminine energy.

She Does What's Exciting to Her

A femme fatale is not average, nor does she settle for an average lifestyle. Sitting at home on the couch all day with the remote control in hand, while binge-watching Netflix with a tub of ice cream next to her—spoon to mouth, dressed untidily in her old pj's is not her fantasy of excitement (even when she's on her own). Instead, you will find her dressed in the most fashionable gym clothes, hitting the treadmill while listening to high-energy music.

She loves to do those things that leave her feeling enthused, pumped up for action, and brimming with health and vitality. You might find her afterward enjoying a sauna session while planning her day out methodically. Sure, she watches movies and enjoys timeout sessions on her couch, but it is not a lifestyle nor is it a daily habit. It is not something that she would jump at doing at the first given opportunity.

Addressing her physical needs is a priority because she knows the results that will manifest from hitting the treadmill more often than not. Doing things like planning weekends away at her favorite retreat spas, taking hikes, exploring new dining venues, and attending social calls with people to widen her professional network—while working at her goals. Those are the things that will amount to something for her in life.

They lead to new opportunities and broaden her horizons. She is also not one for sitting on the couch in her comfort zone. Trying out new things is adventurous and moving toward what she wants by making choices that make her have meaningful priorities. Taking care of her health, body, mind, and spirit is part of her daily self-care routine.

Get Moving With Exercise

Getting healthy means getting your body moving regularly. It's great for your entire well-being: body, mind, and soul. Regular exercise oxygenates your cells, relieves stress, tones your muscles, and maintains healthy joints. When you exercise consistently and follow a healthy lifestyle in combination with regular exercise, it will also reduce your chances of developing any chronic health issues. Let's face it: Staying active is an important lifestyle to follow. You will undoubtedly feel great every day, getting fresh air while stretching your tired muscles and joints. Exercising will also make you feel radiant from the inside out.

Shaking off excess energy caused by stress and spending long hours working is a wonderful way of starting and ending your day. What's more, when you exercise regularly, your body produces hormones that make you feel great and put you in a great mood. These hormones are called endorphins and they are released directly into your body during a workout. So, put on those sneakers and sweatbands and download your favorite music to enjoy the full benefits of connecting your body, mind, and soul this way (DiGiulio, 2021).

Follow a Healthy Diet

What you put into your body matters. Your body is not a machine. It requires to be fueled with specific nutrition to benefit your vital organs, tissues, cells, and nervous systems. Food is the source of energy that can leave you feeling either great or depleted, lethargic, and bloated. Opting for a lighter, healthier diet is the way to go. Be sure to choose carefully what you are putting inside your body. Cut down drastically on your sugar intake and foods that are high in fats. Also, cut out on eating too much red meat.

Choose vegan alternatives for healthy protein, and eat more probiotic and plant-based food to stay healthy naturally. Also, add superfoods and fermented foods such as kefir to your diet, and opt for dairy alternatives. When it comes to desserts, you can also opt for dairy-free desserts instead of going for heavy full-cream ones.

The body needs regular doses of water (at least eight glasses a day) so that it can function efficiently. The more you reach out for water instead of soft drinks, alcohol, or other beverages, the better you will satisfy your bodily needs. Your body's entire system—its organs, tissues, and cells—requires water for maximum impact.

Skin Care and Beauty Routine

The beauty of having a structured day filled with healthy routines is to boost your mood and improve the health of your body and mind. Researchers found that consistent self-care routines reduce the chances of suffering from depressive and even bipolar disorders.

This is important because mental health issues also lead to loneliness and unhappiness. It will strip you of your chance of activating your dark feminine energy, especially when things get tough. So, to stay in touch with your inner femme fatale, add an inspiring skin and beauty care ritual to your daily self-care routine.

It will also give you a chance to add one more mindfulness activity to your list while caring for your skin at the same time. Activities that bring you to the present moment act as a buffer against depression and anxiety. When you focus on a beauty routine, you will be unhooking your thoughts from spiraling thinking patterns. This is what increases mindfulness. Feel inspired to throw in a nightly mud pack, face-steaming session, and moisturizing ritual before going to bed. You will also wake up with a rejuvenated skin tone (Migala, 2020).

Taking Care of Yourself Mentally

Mental health is important, especially if you want to stay in top form manifesting your dark feminine energy to remain enigmatic, mysterious, and in control of your life. Checking in with yourself regularly to see how you're doing is important. This includes paying attention to your thoughts, feelings, and emotions. When things get stressful, take a break. Note your feelings every day and pay attention to what is going on inside of you.

If you want to remain productive in your professional life, self-care becomes important, and practicing emotional resilience is just as vital as it will determine your capacity to make sound decisions without unraveling mentally under stress. Journaling, practicing mindfulness, and investing in ongoing learning opportunities tops the list when it comes to keeping your mind sharp, stress-free, and healthy (Anwar, 2021).

Journaling

Journaling regularly will help you stay in touch with how you're coping daily and it will also help you achieve clarity on all matters concerning your life. Strong women are the ones who are paying attention to their thoughts, feelings, and emotions. They are also always planning and maintaining a flow of inspired creativity to keep them happy and thriving.

As you also progress in your meditation and spiritual practice of practicing mindfulness, journal your transformation and make a note of the progress you are making as well as the insights unfolding daily. Journaling is also a great way to reflect on your goals, and the progress you are making in that respect, and fine-tune things as life presents new opportunities and challenges. Remember that a femme fatale wants to stay ahead of her game of life.

This includes coming up with creative solutions for every challenge—journaling helps as it offers an opportunity for self-expression and also venting when things get tough. Journaling offers you a chance to glimpse the truth behind your motivation and it also helps you to develop deeper bonds with yourself. As we've already touched on the importance of doing shadow work on yourself, you can also achieve this in your journal by getting to the core of deep underlying issues related to your mental health (Derisz, 2021).

Mindfulness Meditation

Mindfulness meditation is a great way to train your mind not to be taken over by every thought and feeling that emerges during the day. It will also allow you the space to become more of an observer than sit in judgment of all thoughts and feelings that flash through your mind. Always keep in mind that it is not always easy to control your thoughts. However, you can moderate your reaction to them and you can learn to drop those that are not productive or adding value to your day.

Being an observer of your thoughts and feelings will also help you to regulate your emotions better. Femmes fatales don't throw tantrums based on their running thoughts and emotions. They choose, instead, to assert themselves, they say no to things that they do not want to engage in, and they communicate effectively to reach the best agreements and understanding. To get started with the daily practice of mindfulness meditation, follow the steps below (Wong, 2021):

1. Find a quiet spot.

2. Position yourself comfortably.

3. Ensure there will not be any disruptions.

4. Begin by closing your eyes and focusing on your breathing.

5. Do deep breathing. Inhale and exhale while you clear your mind to pay attention to how you're feeling.

6. Ask yourself: Is there any discomfort in your body or mind?

7. Identify strong emotions and thoughts and just observe them without judgment.

8. Next, allow these thoughts and feelings to leave your awareness by bringing your focus back to your breathing.

9. Keep in mind that we can, through conscious effort, avoid being pulled into every thought and feeling that emerges for us.

10. Begin letting go of negative thoughts and feelings and declare your nonattachment to all of them.

11. Repeat this process for about 15 min. Allow the ebb and flow of your thoughts to enter and leave your mind, and always bring your awareness back to your breathing.

12. This meditation will empower you to better manage your thoughts and reaction to them.

Education

A woman who is investing in her ongoing education is bound to keep moving forward, especially if her studies are aligned with her professional goals. Commit to following a path of continuous education to uplift your life and expand your horizons. Once you get very clear on your vision, you will find it easy to map out an educational goal chart that will see you progress in your personal empowerment journey. It is important to upskill and expand your knowledge if you want to succeed in life.

How to Become a Fascinating Person That Everyone Wants to Know

This is where all the work you've done on your inner transformation starts to take shape and people notice you more profoundly. Once you powerfully manifest your dark feminine energy to bring out more of your irresistible femme fatale qualities, you will soon become a people's magnet. Authentic power is an illuminating force of inspiration. Being fascinating includes exploring the world, traveling, discovering exotic and interesting new places to hang out, and independently expressing yourself.

When you are independent and naturally curious without socialized limiting beliefs standing in your way, you can boldly go out into the world, explore it, and also manifest your mission. Femmes fatales love to shine their light of wisdom, knowledge, and adventure in the world. They are not afraid of being noticed for their original contribution.

Seeing the world through travel is an incredibly eye-opening experience. A femme fatale has the air of an experienced, well-traveled person. But even if you don't have the time or money to travel the world, you can still come across as well-traveled. Most people don't even fully explore the city they live in themselves. If you can travel abroad or across the country, that's best, but even if you can't right now, don't let that stop you. Go out and explore a new part of your town you've never been to. Or, check out that new coffee shop in a trendy neighborhood.

Exploration can happen anywhere. Exploration is important. If you want to manifest what you don't yet have, then you can't just keep going to the same places and doing the same things and expect your life to change. Life changes occur when you become a true adventurer, broaden your horizons, and illuminate your path with new experiences.

CLOSING AFFIRMATION:

I am radiant with the wisdom and clarity that my dark feminine side reveals to me daily.

SECRET #6

How to Have Hypnotically Powerful Body Language and Style

Even though the body appears to be material, it is not. In the deeper reality, your body is a field of energy, transformation, and intelligence.

–Deepak Chopra

Attractiveness Is an Inward Journey

Feeling good about your natural beauty, personality, body language, and how you present who you are to the world is more than enough. When you compare yourself to others, that is when you are being unreasonable. Nobody can live up to unrealistic expectations, so don't even try to measure up to false expectations of yourself. Rather, focus on your natural physical appearance and measure up to the standards that you set for yourself. Be comfortable with your appearance and practice self-love.

Confidence is incredibly attractive. Carrying yourself out confidently in all situations is a winning ticket to being noticed and standing out. Femmes fatales are always confident in all situations. They also take a lot of pride in how they dress, as they recognize the importance of having a fashionable look. Dressing smartly, taking pride in your attire, and using body language when communicating are all also important confidence factors.

Using Appropriate Body Language

Body language is a way of communicating nonverbally to others. We are doing it all the time, whether we are aware of it or not. For example, when you're angry with someone and being confrontational, you might place your hands on your hips. Or, when you're happy and excited, you might use your hands excessively when communicating and expressing your feelings. Body language does have a way of also impacting how people feel about us. If we are moody, unconfident, and unhappy, we may close ourselves up by crossing our arms across our chest. Our facial expressions will also convey these feelings of unhappiness when we don't smile or make eye contact.

This means that you can also use your body language to attract a partner. Body movements, facial expressions, and even the way you dress all can be used to come across as being attractive, interested, and sexy. If your motivation is to attract a partner, then you can use your body language, facial expression, and attire to show off your best qualities, to become seductive, interesting, and open to dating the person. Showing interest doesn't have to be over the top.

The art of seduction should be used subtly, especially when you are just getting to know someone. Aim to come off confident and interesting by using your body language. For example, if you're sitting with your back straight, you can come across as being someone interested in what the other person is saying. It also conveys the message of respect and courtesy, as opposed to slouching and using your hands a lot to distract the person who is speaking to you. Here's a simple, yet effective way of using your body language to attract someone (Adams, 2022):

1.   Sit up straight with your back against a backrest.

2.   Avoid slouching or crossing your legs.

3.   Face the person who is speaking to you.

4.   Keep your hands visible instead of inside your pockets.

5.   You may cross your arms loosely if this makes you feel more comfortable.

6.   Your elbows should be close to your sides.

7.   Maintain eye contact when speaking.

8.   Avoid fidgeting, and smile, be warm and engaging.

9.   Listen and pay attention when the person you're interested in speaks to you.

10. Do make an effort to make a good first impression.

11. You can use your eyes to flirt, hold their gaze, and appear seductive.

12. You can also use your voice to sound appealing.

13. Speak slowly and confidently, and express your thoughts and feelings clearly.

14. Make sure that you're poised and graceful in the use of your body language.

15. Ultimately, aim to be yourself when expressing your views.

Making Eye Contact

Eye contact can be a powerful, seductive way of communicating your attraction to someone. Some say the eyes are the mirrors of a person's soul. Others say that eye contact can convey powerful messages on its own without the need for words. A look or even a glance of admiration in someone's direction can serve as a powerful way of letting someone know that they've caught your attention.

During a conversation, a smiling or flirty set of eyes can also say more than the actual words that you use. You could be saying, "Please pass me the water at the table," while your eyes may be sending electric shocks of sexual attraction at the same time.

If you fail to use your eyes effectively when communicating with others, whether on a one-on-one basis or in a small gathering, you will soon lose the attention of your audience. Making eye contact during any conversation is indicative of a confident and present person.

The triangular method is used to make eye contact without staring into someone's eyes directly all the time. It is an effective way of maintaining eye contact steadily. The method includes looking at one eye at a time, then gazing down to the mouth, and then up again to each eye. Here are more reasons to use striking eye contact when in conversation with anyone (Eatough, 2021):

1. They will remember what you said better because your focus and attention are directly on them.

2. You are showing respect and interest when making eye contact.

3. You are showing charisma and confidence when using your eyes as a nonverbal way of communicating with someone.

4. It shows that you are certain of your ideas, thoughts, and feelings.

5. It displays honesty when communicating with someone.

6. It also improves understanding between people and deepens the level of intimate communication experienced.

7. It can be extremely seductive when you look straight at someone to flirt with them with your eyes as you communicate your romantic and physical attraction to them.

8. It also communicates to others that you are not someone who can be easily manipulated or coerced into doing anything that makes you uncomfortable.

9. Eye contact made regularly also builds more attraction between people.

10. It builds familiarity and rapport between people and makes opening up to each other more comfortable.

Using Your Voice Appropriately

Using your voice is another powerful way of being more confident to convey your message effectively. Confidence by itself is an attractive quality. Being able to articulate your thoughts clearly, confidently, and in a tone that is attractive but not overbearing will strike the right chord with the person who is listening to you. A tone of voice can be either attractive or repulsive.

It all depends on your ability to speak in a tone that is not dull and lifeless but animated, inflected, and controlled. Think of how some voices can just grab your attention immediately, while others don't. A rich expressive tone matched with intelligence, charm, and charisma is not only appealing and effective for communication purposes—it is also seductive and hypnotic!

As you speak, think of the words you are using and get into your message to articulate your thoughts and ideas skillfully. Avoid stumbling over your words when nervous or choosing words that you cannot pronounce properly. Rather, use simple vocabulary to convey a message or idea effectively. Practice makes perfect.

Articulate some of your ideas, thoughts, and feelings to yourself more often and see what an impact that will have when you communicate with others. You will start feeling more at ease when you practice your communication style with yourself first (Beccia, 2020).

Power Poses

Power poses are body postures that will help you feel more powerful, assertive, and in control. When you assume a specific power pose, it signals to your brain that you are feeling strong, confident, and in charge. It also boosts levels of confidence and reduces anxiety and feelings of insecurity. When we act confidently by taking on nonverbal powerful postures, it also makes us feel like we can do anything that we set our mind on accomplishing.

So, when you are facing obstacles or daunting situations, take on a power pose to reduce feeling powerless and increase your femme fatale presence with the firm intention of overcoming and even overpowering people who are being dominant. It is a nonverbal way of saying, "I am tough, and I got this!" Here are some power poses to get you started (Poised & Professional, n.d.):

1. **The Wonder Woman pose:** This is by far the most well-known power pose used today to convey strong dominance and control in work or personal situations. It shows assertiveness and also conveys the message that you are totally in charge of the situation. Stand with your feet apart. Then lift your chest and head up while placing your hands firmly on your hips.

2. **The salutation pose:** Think of this pose as a self-affirming pose that can invoke feelings of positivity, self-love, and presence. Outstretch your arms and give your body a good stretch by lifting your chest and your head at the same time. Your palms should face the sun. Do this often during the day to energize yourself and invoke feelings of personal power.

3. **The victory pose:** This is a lovely pose to use daily when out exercising or stretching your body. You can also use this pose when involved in team exercises. Imagine an athlete that has crossed the finish line, raising their arms

in victory. A celebratory pose that can be used in work or personal situations conveys a possible and confident message of achieving victory.

4. **Table leaning pose:** This is another power pose to use when in a meeting or talking to anyone while standing. Simply lean forward on the table by placing the palms of your hands on the table. It is a confident pose and conveys a message of assertiveness and attentiveness at the same time.

Discovering Your Dark Feminine Style

It is going to be fun discovering your fashion style when manifesting your dark feminine energy. A great place to begin is to find your style icons—women that you admire for their taste in fashion. Take a closer look at the type of clothing they wear and pay attention to how they coordinate their dress. Also, subscribe to fashion magazines to see what the latest trends are. You can also follow your favorite brands and fashion influences on social media. Maybe some of the new trends may interest you. The idea is to get out of the comfort zone of your current dressing style and explore new ways of dressing up.

You should ideally choose a fashion that flatters your body type and also makes you feel comfortable, sexy, and confident. This will further help you to get in touch with your dark feminine side. What is important is that you define what dark feminine means to you in your fashion style. The colors and styles that you choose, including the cuts, must ultimately appeal to you. Experiment with new types of fashion to see how they best suit you. Above all, have fun discovering your own unique dark feminine style. Here are some extra tips for finding your style icon:

1. Identify women who you admire for their fashion style.

2. Check out their pictures on the internet and pay attention to their choice of clothing, accessories, makeup, and hairstyles.

3. Identify their choice of fashion for different events. For example, pay attention to how they dress casually, formally, and when out with their partners.

4. Use these ideas to revamp your wardrobe by assessing how you can improve in all different areas of grooming and fashion.

5. Follow them on social media to stay abreast of their evolving fashion style.

6. Be experimentative until you develop your own fashion signature in how you dress, groom your hair, and wear your makeup.

CLOSING AFFIRMATION:

I am confident in my dark feminine style and always present an authentic version of who I am to the world!

SECRET #7

Seduction—How to Make Men Adore You

Your greatest power in seduction is your ability to turn away, to make others come after you, delaying their satisfaction.

–Robert Greene

Show Them You're a High-Value Woman

A femme fatale is a high-value woman because she puts herself first, does not compromise on what is important to her in a relationship, and knows what she wants and expects nothing less. She also sets healthy boundaries accordingly. A high-value woman today is regarded as someone who knows what she is deserving of and expects to get it. She is determined and wily and loves pursuing things that are important to her. The same rule applies to her love life.

So, if you have low self-esteem and feel needy and are clingy when someone you fancy gives you a little attention, you will be sending the message to them that you do not value yourself enough. In today's cat-and-mouse game of relationships, playing hard to get does come across as being a high-value woman. Men love the chase and they want to invest their time and energy in a relationship with a partner who sees herself as high value.

When you are easy to get hold of telephonically, always willing to engage in a conversation with someone who may be interested in dating you, it sends the signal that you don't care much about yourself and that you will be willing to accept anything fast to get involved with this person. A femme fatale, on the other hand, will pretend that she didn't notice being noticed by someone she likes and is mutually attracted to.

Instead, she will ignore the attention but not dismiss it entirely—just enough to leave a hint of interest. That is done deliberately, to keep the person wondering if they do have at least half a chance to move things forward with her. A femme fatale won't be waiting around for a call from the person who she is mutually attracted to. Instead, she simply gets on with life and wishes them luck in winning her favor.

A femme fatale knows what she wants and expects in a relationship. This is why she is not going to get all flattered and worked up with excitement when someone she fancies notices her. She only gets serious with a suitor when she senses or knows with a great deal of certainty that the person to whom she is attracted is on her wavelength. In other words, there must be mutual attraction and like-mindedness. It's not that she is a snob.

It's just that she respects and values herself that much more than the average woman looking for a partner. A femme fatale wants to have her ideal partner next to her and if she doesn't find the ideal partner soon, all the better to take her time and enjoy more of the single life. Here's a list of the traits that high-value women display. See how many you can tick off that resonate with you (Roman, 2021).

1.   Highly independent.

2.   Loves and respects herself.

3. Enjoys time spent on her own.

4. Does not feel lonely, but comfortable in her own space.

5. Embraces both her light and dark feminine energy.

6. She knows that she deserves so much more in life and keeps going after it.

7. Has high standards and expectations of others.

8. She is super-confident.

9. Takes pride in her grooming.

10. She enjoys setting meaningful goals.

11. She has a great sense of humor and enjoys a good laugh often.

12. She is kind and emotionally stable.

13. She is dependable, reliable, and follows a code of ethics and integrity that is admirable.

14. She does not put up with lies.

15. She keeps drama out of her space and prefers simplicity and straightforwardness.

16. She cannot be manipulated.

17. She is spiritual and trusts her intuition.

18. She is highly committed to her personal growth.

19. She takes pride in her work.

20. She is an effective communicator.

Decoding the Male Psyche

Now that you know what a high-value woman is, you must aim to achieve being one yourself. If you were clingy, needy, or codependent in the past, it does not mean that you should continuously follow this trajectory in life. It is time to shift gears and earn the respect you deserve by ticking all the above boxes to own the traits of being a high-value woman. In your desire to be a high-value woman, taking more interest in the male psyche will empower you further.

This means that you must know and accept that he will want to impress you all the time, to be the hero in your life. What does this mean exactly? High-value women are looking for partners, friends, and a lover who they can depend on. So, being the hero may seem like a very shallow quality to accept. However, the male psyche is such that all men aspire to earn the hero title with the woman they desire to be with.

A man is driven biologically to protect the people they care about. This means they will go out of their way to make you feel loved, safe, and protected (by nature—not to say that all men will desire to express this for sure). It makes them feel good and you will enjoy it too once you allow them to do their manly thing in your favor. It does not make you less independent as a femme fatale.

What it does is make you more needed by the man who wants to impress you with their manliness. The best advice is to let them stick up for you and invest in their relationship with you as your hero. It is a sure sign of their commitment, love, affection, and loyalty to you. Men take that seriously, and so should you. Here are some ways to trigger the hero in your man (Burgemeester, 2022).

1. Compliment him genuinely.

2. Praise him in front of other people.

3. Support him in his goals.

4. Let him do manly jobs.

5. Consult him for his opinion.

6. Reach out to him for help.

7. Be vulnerable with him by expressing your emotional side.

8. Don't be needy by always reaching out to him as if you're afraid of losing him.

9. Give him some space to be on his own.

10. Let him know that you're happy to be with him.

The Attractive Quality of Confidence

Now that you understand the male psyche, you can give him what he needs without being a doormat for him to wipe his feet on. Whip up some dark feminine energy and remember to be your wonderful unique, mysterious self who is always on the go in her life. Don't always be available for him. Delay taking his calls all the time, and doesn't always say yes to everything that he wants to do.

Be a challenge by manifesting your inner femme fatale and while you're giving him what he wants, keep it subtle. He must not know that you understand him better than he thinks. For example, you know that the hero in him would love compliments, so don't come across as if you're trying too hard. Give him genuine compliments about the things that you love about him and appreciate.

Femmes fatales don't play games with men as a rule. That's because when they are interested in a man as a partner, they commit to them equally. This is also why it is important to them to keep their communication open, direct, and unashamedly authentic.

Femmes fatales have high standards and they communicate their expectations and standards directly to their partner to ensure they are understood and will not be setting themselves up for disappointment. If you have pet peeves that trigger you in a bad way, then communicate this with your partner upfront to avoid being negatively triggered. For example, if you detest your phone calls not being returned timeously, let them know.

How to Make Men Attracted to You

It is a wonderful thing to be yourself when attracting your ideal partner. Femmes fatales are confident women, and since they are already in touch with their femininity (dark and light), they know how to turn each one on to keep the attraction going. Being flirty and fun comes with the territory of being a femme fatale. Keep a sense of humor when you're out with the man you're attracted to, make jokes when appropriate, speak from your heart about the things that interest you, and stimulate interesting conversations that are of interest to you both.

Take an interest in his profession by asking questions, and also take an interest in the things that he occupies his pastime with. Find a balance when engaging with a potential partner as both a friend and a love interest. Being yourself is key to attracting a man—it is a simple yet profound formula for success and personal fulfillment. Follow what you believe and above everything else be comfortable.

How to Stop Being Manipulated for Good and Step Into Your Power

It is not difficult to sense when you're being manipulated by someone. Femmes fatales are good at trusting their instincts and they do pay attention to men and anyone else when engaging. Manipulation can sometimes be subtle, but it's not hard to miss. You will feel like the other person is trying to control you. It may also come across as if they want to use you for something or the other.

When you sense an imbalance of power in your association with others, then be warned that they are using a manipulation tactic to get you to do their bidding for them. Sometimes, manipulators may also be suffering from a personality disorder, like narcissistic personality disorder.

Their tactic may be to love bomb you at first to win your admiration and favor, only to turn on you later once they know that they have you hooked. This is also why it is important to manifest your dark feminine energy. A strong and independent woman will not succumb easily to manipulation. Instead, they will boldly step into their power to assert themselves, strongly if needed. Another tactic employed by a manipulator is to make you feel guilty, or use your weaknesses to hurt you so that they feel they have some kind of power over you.

Manipulators are generally people with low self-esteem issues. They feel the need to be in control of others to get what they want. A strong dark feminine energy trait is, therefore, not to wear their heart on their sleeves and to take their time to get to know people, instead of rushing in too quickly.

Don't be quick to chase men or get carried away with their flattery. It is always best to have your feet firmly on the ground, rooted in the things that are important to you personally and professionally, instead of in the sky conjuring up fantasies of being swept off your feet. Getting to know people takes time and effort. Someone willing to put in the effort to get to know you back is a better option than anyone who wants quick results from you, so much so that they will resort to excessive flattery.

Getting people to do what you want is a matter of effectively communicating your needs, expectations, and desires to them when entering into any kind of relationship—be it personal or professional. Manipulation that is based on winning hearts and minds is not damaging as the type used by narcissists and others who want to exert control over people by using cruel, unfair, and sometimes very damaging tactics.

Never Lower Your Standards

There's a simple rule to follow: As long as your standards are reasonable, never lower them. Your standards make up your expectations of how you would love to be treated in a relationship. If those standards are not met, then you will not be entirely happy staying in such a relationship. This is why it is always wise to ensure that your standards are being met, by communicating them effectively upfront when getting involved with someone in a new relationship.

We all know that no one is perfect. Standards should include things like the same philosophies that you believe in and not things like where the person comes from, what their race is, or the color of their hair. However, when there is a clash of personal beliefs and expectations in a relationship, then your chances of being happy with this partner will diminish until it reaches a point where you will feel deeply unhappy and frustrated.

A mistake would be to lower your standards just to find and be with Mr. Right. If someone is not the right fit for you, then don't waste your time. This is also why it is important to have clarity on what you want to experience and find in a relationship with someone else. Getting into a relationship with someone based only on physical attraction is also another mistake to make.

Getting to know a potential partner and taking your time to establish mutual standards or expectations are important. You may not always have the same feelings on specific issues, but as long as your core expectations are being met and there are similarities in your personal beliefs, things may still work out between the two of you. Your standards can also make up your boundaries.

When the opposite occurs and there is a clash in beliefs, expectations, and boundaries, then it would be best to move on from the relationship completely. Walking away can save you time, energy, and frustration. Remember that there is a difference between being realistic and living in a fairy tale.

Also, remember that not everyone is going to meet your expectations or be willing to meet your standards. However, it is always better to have standards in place, so that you will not be disrespected and start feeling resentful. It helps to have some kind of foundation in place before overcommitting to a relationship or getting involved with people who do not meet your standards.

CLOSING AFFIRMATION:

I am inspired to live a life worthy of high-value women, deserving of love and lasting happiness.

Conclusion

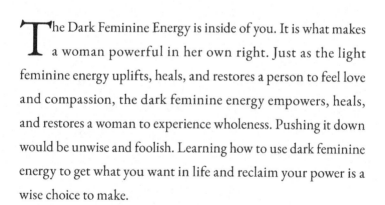

The Dark Feminine Energy is inside of you. It is what makes a woman powerful in her own right. Just as the light feminine energy uplifts, heals, and restores a person to feel love and compassion, the dark feminine energy empowers, heals, and restores a woman to experience wholeness. Pushing it down would be unwise and foolish. Learning how to use dark feminine energy to get what you want in life and reclaim your power is a wise choice to make.

The reason I wrote this book was to help other women heal from feelings of inadequacy and perceived lack, just as I have healed from them. Coming to full terms with this incredible and magnetic force within will liberate you from those lower energy feelings and it will restore you to feel a wholeness that you've not experienced before.

Denying its voice of love and wisdom will be a great mistake to make. Some of the best qualities that women possess as you've discovered in this book are those that emulate dark feminine energy. These qualities are assertiveness, determination, resilience, leadership, fortitude, and independence. Women are as capable as men are today when it comes to manifesting their goals, achieving success, and living the life of their dreams.

I've shared many wonderful stories and insights from other women who've stepped into their power in this book with you. Those stories are all true and inspiring. It is only because of their ability to manifest the dark feminine traits that led to their ability to overcome the many setbacks and hurdles they faced in their life's journey.

Just as they have, so can you. Every woman has it in her to overcome all the setbacks and challenges that come her way, when she lets out her inner femme fatale. We all have our own version of femme fatale within us—the ability to conquer our fears and be a trailblazer in our own right. The tide has turned for women in the modern era as they've taken on important leadership and specialist positions across all industries.

It was not always this way in the past. Women have always been let down by people due to a lack of understanding of the dual nature of feminine power. When women are strong, assertive, independent, and sexually liberated, they are misjudged. If they are down on luck, they are misjudged. If they are torn between choosing a career or a marriage partner, they are misjudged.

However, as you've discovered in the pages of this book, what matters is not how others judge women, but how they judge themselves. What matters is how she feels about her inner femme fatale that emerges from the ashes of her past mistakes. Is she going to empower herself more with this energy, or will she go back to playing small and accepting mediocrity?

The power of choice always resides within you, to choose appropriately for your life. Whatever happened to you in the past is nothing to be ashamed of anymore. You now know the true power that lies within you. Rebel if you must, and by all means go after everything that you desire in life. You are worth it!

96 Powerful Affirmations & Self Discovery Prompts to Unlock Your Dark Feminine Energy

Access your additional 96 affirmation and prompts here by using the QR code below.

References

Anwar, B. (2021, November 24). *Why is mental health important?* Talkspace. https://www.talkspace.com/ blog/why-is-mental-health-important/

Beccia, C. (2022, October 31). *10 simple ways to make your voice sound more attractive.* Medium. https:// psiloveyou.xyz/10-simple-ways-to-make-your-voice-sound-more-attractive-e953d6917f1e

Branden, N. (1994). *The six pillars of self-esteem.* Bantam.

Burgemeester, A. (2022, January 6). *15 ways to trigger hero instinct in men.* The Narcissistic Life. https:// thenarcissisticlife.com/hero-instinct-in-men/

Cherry, K. (2023, April 14). *How to deal with the fear of failure.* Verywell Mind. https://www.verywellmind. com/what-is-the-fear-of-failure-5176202

Chowdhury, M. R. (2019, April 9). *The neuroscience of gratitude and how it affects anxiety & grief.* Positive Psychology. https://positivepsychology.com/neuroscience-of-gratitude/

Derisz, R. (2021, February 4). *A guide to journaling for spiritual growth and self-development.* MindThatEgo. https://www.mindthatego.com/journaling-for-spiritual-growth/

DiGiulio, S. (2021, October 6). *Self-care tips during the coronavirus pandemic.* Everyday Health. https://www.everydayhealth.com/wellness/top-self-care-tips-for-being-stuck-at-home-during-the-coronavirus-pandemic/

Eatough, E. (2021, September 9). *Eye contact is important (crucial really) in communication.* BetterUp. https://www.betterup.com/blog/why-is-eye-contact-important

F&F Team. (n.d.). *50+ quotes to manifest anything you want.* Fortune & Frame. https://fortuneandframe.com/blogs/news/manifestation-quotes

Goodreads. (n.d.). *Quotable quote.* https://www.goodreads.
com/quotes/9069867-what-you-resist-not-only-
persists-but-will-grow-in

Griffiths, E. (2017, August 10). *Halle Berry reveals she once
lived in a homeless shelter.* HELLO! https://www.
hellomagazine.com/celebrities/2017081041443/
halle-berry-homeless-shelter/

Gurukal, L. (n.d.). *How to harness the goddess energy of
Kali Ma.* LEELA.
https://www.leelagurukul.com/blog/how-to-
harness-goddess-energy-of-kali

Harper's BAZAAR Staff. (2017, March 8). *75 empowering
feminist quotes from inspiring women.* Harper's
BAZAAR. https://www.harpersbazaar.com/
culture/features/a4056/empowering-female-quotes/

Hutto, C. (n.d.). *38 motivational quotes from successful
women we admire.* InHerSight. https://
www.inhersight.com/blog/women-to-know/
successful-women-quotes

Jay, S. (2022, July 18). *How to embrace dark feminine energy
& unleash your power.* Revoloon. https://revoloon.
com/shanijay/dark-feminine-energy

Jessica from San Diego. (2012, May 18). *Coco Chanel.* The MY HERO Project. https://myhero.com/C_Chanel_dnhs_US_2012_ul

Juma, N. (2022, June 29). *Insightful Arianna Huffington quotes on American culture.* Everyday Power. https://everydaypower.com/arianna-huffington-quotes/

Keithley, Z. (2022, March 7). *9 guided meditations for manifesting your desires.* Zanna Keithley. https://zannakeithley.com/guided-meditations-for-manifesting/

Migala, J. (2020, April 30). *5 ways a skin-care routine benefits mental health.* Everyday Health. https://www.everydayhealth.com/skin-beauty/5-reasons-maintaining-a-skin-care-routine-is-good-for-your-mental-health/

Nast, C. (2022, May 26). *How to manifest your goals with the help of the moon cycle.* Vogue India. https://www.vogue.in/beauty/content/how-to-manifest-your-goals-with-the-help-of-the-moon-cycle

Nast, C. (2023, June 2). *The rise of dark feminine energy is a reminder for women to reclaim their power.* Vogue India. https://www.vogue.in/content/

dark-feminine-energy-is-a-reminder-for-women-to-reclaim-their-power

The National Archives. (n.d.). *Florence Nightingale.* https://www.nationalarchives.gov.uk/education/resources/florence-nightingale

One Accord Physical Therapy. (n.d.). *Here's why you should add massages to your self-care routine.* https://www.oneaccordpt.com/blog/heres-why-you-should-add-massages-to-your-self-care-routine

Poised & Professional. (n.d.). *5 power poses to kickstart your confidence.* https://poisedandprofessional.com/2019/02/5-power-poses-to-kickstart-your-confidence

Quora. (2011, November 29). *What is a good summary of Oprah's philosophy of life?* Forbes. https://www.forbes.com/sites/quora/2011/11/29/what-is-a-good-summary-of-oprahs-philosophy-of-life/?sh=1806521529f2

Regan, S. (2021, June 17). *You've heard of the law of attraction — but how about the law of vibration?* Mindbodygreen. https://www.mindbodygreen.com/articles/law-of-vibration

Richardson, T. C. (2022, December 23). *18 signs you're experiencing a synchronicity (and not just coincidence).* Mindbodygreen. https://www.mindbodygreen.com/articles/synchronicities

Roman, C. (2021, September 8). *27 traits of a high-value woman that separates her from everyone else.* Hack Spirit. https://hackspirit.com/traits-of-a-high-value-woman/

Salaky, K. (2017, August 9). *11 scientific ways to make yourself look and feel more attractive.* Insider. https://www.insider.com/ways-to-look-feel-more-attractive-confident-2017-8#give-yourself-a-pep-talk-4

Self Help Motivation. (2021, November 25). *9 amazing effects of visualization on the brain.* https://selfhelp-motivation.net/effects-of-visualization-on-the-brain/?expand_article=1

Sharma, R. (2022, July 20). *Must I lean into my "dark feminine energy"?* Vice. https://www.vice.com/en/article/jgpmmx/what-is-dark-feminine-energy-tiktok

Sicinski, A. (2009, April 13). *The universal law of cause and effect and its impact on your life.* IQ Matrix Blog. https://blog.iqmatrix.com/law-of-cause-effect

Smith, I. (2020, July 30). *How does trauma affect the brain? - and what it means for you.* Whole Wellness Therapy. https://www.wholewellnesstherapy.com/post/trauma-and-the-brain

Spector, N. (2018, January 10). *Smiling can trick your brain into happiness — and boost your health.* NBC News. https://www.nbcnews.com/better/health/smiling-can-trick-your-brain-happiness-boost-your-health-ncna822591

Wergin, A. (2020, July 22). *Water is essential to your body.* Mayo Clinic Health System. https://www.mayoclinichealthsystem.org/hometown-health/speaking-of-health/water-essential-to-your-body

Whitener, S. (2022, January 25). *Council post: How to uncover unconscious barriers and manifest your desires.* Forbes. https://www.forbes.com/sites/forbescoachescouncil/2022/01/25/how-to-uncover-unconscious-barriers-and-manifest-your-desires/

Willard, C. (2019, January 17). *6 ways to practice mindful eating.* Mindful. https://www.mindful.org/6-ways-practice-mindful-eating/

Williams, S. (2023, April 11). *Positive energy quotes for healing*. Everyday Power. https://everydaypower. com/positive-energy-quotes/

Wong, C. (2021, April 8). *Mindfulness meditation*. Verywell Mind. https://www.verywellmind.com/mindfulness-meditation-88369

Wright, J. (2022, January 16). *30 shadow work prompts for healing and growth*. PureWow. https://www. purewow.com/wellness/shadow-work-prompts

Made in the USA
Las Vegas, NV
12 December 2023